Little Miss Mu

A Pantomime

Paul Reakes

Samuel French – London
New York – Sydney – Toronto – Hollywood

CHARACTERS

Little Miss Muffet (Molly)
Granfer Fuddlewick
Dame Dolly Drinkup, landlady of the *Fillet Inn*
Jasper Grasper, a travelling showman
Flip |
Flop | his "Artistes"
Captain Jack Dauntless, of the *Pretty Polly*
The Spider (Princess Valtina)
Morac, an evil witch
The Good Fairy
A Gorilla
King Valentine of Valador
Queen Valtora
Chorus of Villagers, Fishermen, Barmaids, Children,
Sailors and Demons

SYNOPSIS OF SCENES

ACT I

ACT II

MUSIC PLOT

ACT I

1.	Song	Chorus
2.	Song and Dance	Molly, Granfer and chorus
3.	Comedy Song	Dame Drinkup
4.	Sand Dance	Flip and Flop
5.	Song	Jack and chorus
6.	Rustic Dance	Chorus
7.	Duet	Jack and Molly
8.	Song and Dance	Dame, Jack, Molly and Spider
9.	Song	Jack, Molly, Dame, Granfer, children and chorus

ACT II

10.	Song	Chorus
11.	Hornpipe	Granfer and sailors
12.	Song	Children
13.	Song	Jack, Molly, Spider and Chorus
14.	Demon Dance	Demons
15.	Song and Dance	Good Fairy
16.	Comedy Song	Dame Drinkup and Jasper Grasper
17.	Gorilla Dance	Gorilla and Dame Drinkup
18.	Song	All
19.	Sing-a-long	Dame, Flip, Flop and audience
20.	Finale Reprise	All

A licence issued by Samuel French Ltd to perform this play does NOT include permission to use any copyright music in the performance. The notice printed below on behalf of the Performing Right Society should be carefully read.

The following statement concerning the use of music is printed here on behalf of the Performing Right Society Ltd, by whom it was supplied

The Permission of the owner of the performing right in copyright music must be obtained before any public performance may be given, whether in conjunction with a play or sketch or otherwise, and this permission is just as necessary for amateur performances as for professional. The majority of copyright musical works (other than oratorios, musical plays and similar dramatico-musical works) are controlled in the British Commonwealth by the PERFORMING RIGHT SOCIETY LTD, 29–33 BERNERS STREET, LONDON W1P 4AA.

The Society's practice is to issue licences authorizing the use of its repertoire to the proprietors of premises at which music is publicly performed, or, alternatively, to the organizers of musical entertainments, but the Society does not require payment of fees by performers as such. Producers or promoters of plays sketches, etc., at which music is to be performed, during or after the play or sketch, should ascertain whether the premises at which their performances are to be given are covered by a licence issued by the Society, and if they are not, should make application to the Society for particulars as to the fee payable.

PRODUCTION NOTES

Staging
The pantomime offers opportunities for elaborate staging, but can be produced quite simply if facilities and funds are limited. There are seven full stage sets:
Outside the *Fillet Inn*
A Glade in the Forest
Dame Drinkup's Parlour
The Deck of the *Pretty Polly*
The Seashore of Valador
Morac's Dark Tower
Transformation (this scene can be used for the Finale)

All these scenes are interlinked with tabs or frontcloth scenes.

The Wallpapering Scene must be a well-rehearsed "slap-stick" routine. The choice of comic business is left to the individual producer. Lots of fun with "crazy foam" paste, stubborn rolls of paper, etc. A protective stage cloth is advisable for this scene.

The Magic Wand is broken during each performance so a good supply is necessary. Please save a special lighting effect (strobe if possible) for when the power of the wand is used.

The Gorilla in the Birthday Cake is optional, but can be a funny and surprise addition to the Finale. Mounted on a trolley, the "cake" is a large box or drum big enough to conceal the Gorilla and decorated to look like icing with candles, buttons, etc. It has a thin paper top which the Gorilla can easily burst through.

CHARACTERS AND COSTUMES

Little Miss Muffet (principal girl) is a petite, pretty young woman who is never soppy or simpering. Her costume should be picturesque and simple. Finale costume.

Granfer Fuddlewick is a comical ancient rustic with an infectious cackle. He is toothless with wispy, white hair and beard. In Act I he wears a rustic smock, battered hat and side-button gaiters. In Act II he wears an outsize naval uniform with enormous epaulettes and a huge cocked hat.

Dame Drinkup is a blousy, buxom pub landlady. All her costumes should be outrageous and funny. In Act I she wears her landlady outfit, a frilly dress and hat for the picnic and a comic fluorescent overall for the wallpapering scene. For Act II her costume is a ludicrous mixture of gym mistress and nautical with "Union Jack" knickers. Finale costume.

Jasper Grasper is an old-style "ham" actor who revels in melodramatic villainy. He has fallen on hard times and his cloak is patched and his top hat dented. After the shipwreck in Act II he wears long combinations, his top hat and a short grass skirt.

Flip and Flop are a daft but lovable duo. They are involved in plenty of slapstick and audience participation. In Act I they wear ill-fitting troubadour costumes, fezzes and nightshirts, comic overalls and big flat caps for the wallpapering scene. In Act II they wear comic nautical attire.

Captain Jack Dauntless (principal boy) is a heroic, young sea captain with a great personality and a smashing pair of legs! He wears the principal boy's version of a blue eighteenth-century captain's uniform with lots of gold braid and a tricorn hat. Finale uniform.

The Spider (child's part) is really **Princess Valtina** who has been transformed by a wicked witch. Despite this handicap she still speaks and behaves like a royal princess. The costume and make-up should be in no way frightening to the children of the audience. A "cute", cartoon spider is the desired effect, but please remember that easy movement and speech is essential and a quick change is necessary towards the end of Act II. It is advisable to have the costume ready and in use well before the actual performance. After the transformation scene, Princess Valtina appears in magnificent robes and a sparkling crown.

Morac, the Witch is the nasty to end all nasties! Her costume, head-dress and make-up should be magnificently evil and out of this world.

The Gorilla only appears in Act II and provides lots of comic monkey business. A standard gorilla costume. In the sing-a-long scene he wears a footman's coat with a "dicky" front and a glittering top hat and bow tie for the Finale.

The Good Fairy (child's part) is still only a learner but she helps as best as she can. A traditional fairy costume with the addition of an "L" plate on her back. For the Finale this is replaced by a tiny pair of wings.

King Valentine and **Queen Valtora** only appear in Act II. They are first seen in ragged robes, but after the transformation scene they appear in magnificent robes and crowns.

The Children are a likeable gang of little mischief makers. They are involved in plenty of the action and musical numbers. In Act I they wear picturesque, rustic costumes. In Act II they can wear either Victorian-style sailor suits or white T-shirts and shorts with "*HMS Pretty Polly*" printed across their chests.

The Demons are a bunch of nasties who specialize in weird dances and fiendish cackles. Their costumes, wigs and make-up should be very ghoulish. Can be played by children or female dancers.

The Chorus are villagers, fishermen, barmaids and sailors with costumes appropriate to their calling. All participate in the action and musical numbers.

Other titles by Paul Reakes in French's Acting Editions include:

Santa In Space a Christmas pantomime adventure

Bang, You're Dead! (one act play)

Mantrap (one act play)

ACT I

SCENE 1

Outside the "Fillet Inn", Periwinkle-on-Sea

The "Fillet Inn" is very prominent L. *It has a practical front door and a large hanging signboard. There are fishermen's cottages* R. *Up* C *are steps leading to a raised walk and the harbour wall. The backcloth shows the sea, sky and fishing boats. A table and benches are set below the inn door*

At rise of the CURTAIN, *villagers and fishermen are discovered singing and making merry. The fishermen are seated around the table. Drinking with them is old Granfer Fuddlewick*

1. Song (Chorus)

After the song, Granfer and the fishermen bang their empty tankards on the table and shout

Granfer
Fishermen } *(together)* ALE! ALE! Bring us more ALE!

They cheer as:

A troupe of pretty barmaids emerge from the inn carrying trays filled with tankards. They serve the fishermen with ale

Granfer *(squeaking at a barmaid and banging his empty tankard)* ALE! 'ERE, MISSY! Bring oi a full 'un! Oi be proper parched, oi be!
1st Barmaid Sorry Granfer. You can't have any more.
Granfer *(agog)* Eh?!
2nd Barmaid We've been told to serve you *one* tankard a day and one tankard only!
Granfer *(in horror)* One tankard!
Barmaids One tankard!
Granfer Who said zo?
3rd Barmaid Dame Drinkup, the landlady.
Granfer *(furious)* BAH! Drat the old dragon! She can't do this to oi! One tankard a day! Oi ... oi'll dry up!
Large Fisherman We wish you would!

He and his cronies roar with laughter. Granfer, enraged, gets to his feet and moves to the fisherman

Granfer Be you lookin' fer a fight, sonny! Come on! Put up yer mitts! *(He spars up and down in front of the fisherman)* Come on! Oi'll zort ee out! You big bag o' wind, you!
Fisherman *(rising with mock terror)* Oo! I'm scared!

He places his hand on Granfer's forehead and holds him at arm's length while the old man "punches" at thin air. Everyone roars with laughter

Granfer (*punching away*) Stand still, ye varmit! Stand still an' fight, I zay! Stand yer ground like a man!

Little Miss Muffet (Molly) enters from the inn and moves down to Granfer and the Fisherman

Fisherman (*still holding Granfer off*) Hello, Miss Muffet.
Molly What are you doing?
Fisherman 'Tis Rocky Four, ere! 'E ain't 'alf giving me a hidin'!

He and his mates bellow with laughter. By now Granfer is exhausted and has slowed down to "slow-motion" punching

Molly (*sternly to the Fisherman*) That's enough! You've had your fun. Let him go!
Fisherman Anything you say, Miss Muffet!

He takes his hand away and Granfer promptly falls flat on his face. All laugh. Molly helps Granfer to his feet

(*Turning to the crowd*) Cor! I'm black and blue all over!

He doubles over with laughter, presenting his rear. Granfer, in a flash, kicks him in the seat of his pants, sending him to the ground

Granfer Now you be! (*He cackles*) Hee! Hee! Hee!

Everyone laughs as the Fisherman gets to his feet

Fisherman (*rolling up his sleeve*) You fusty old fossil! (*He makes for Granfer*) I'll——
Molly (*stepping in front of him*) No, you won't! You'll drink up and be on your way! (*Planting her hands on her hips firmly*) Now!

The Fisherman backs down and slouches off down R, amid jeering laughter from the crowd

Granfer starts staggering about, clutching his chest. It is obviously a put-on job and fools no-one

Granfer Oo! Oo! Oi be feelin' faint! 'Tis me ole ticker! Me 'eart! Me 'eart!
Molly (*with a wink at a barmaid*) Quick! Fetch him a drink——
Granfer (*making a very quick recovery*) Ar!
Molly —of water!
Granfer Bah!

All laugh

Oh, don't *you* be 'ard on oi, Miss Muffet! Don't be like that aunty o' yourn, ole Dolly Drinkup! She'll only let oi 'ave one tankard a day! An' me an ole-age perisher ... oi mean, pensioner! 'Tis proper wicked, 'tis!
Molly I'm sorry, Granfer, but she *is* the landlady and her word is law.
Granfer Bah! She be a right old niggle-knickers! She makes Darth Vader (*or popular TV villain*) look like Andy Pandy!
Molly She's been very kind to me and I love her very much. Aunt Dolly and the dear old *Fillet Inn* are all I've got in the world.
Granfer Oh, Miss Muffet! Oi'd marry ee meself an' take ee away from all this if it weren't fer one thing.

Molly What's that?

Granfer Me ole dad says oi be too young to get wed!

Molly (*smiling*) Thank you for the offer anyway. (*She kisses him on the cheek*)

Granfer (*squirming with delight*) Cooo! That refreshes the parts others beers cannot reach! (*To Molly*) Can oi 'ave a drink now?

Molly No!

Granfer Oh! . . . Fish'ooks!

Female Villager Have you got a boyfriend, Miss Muffet?

Molly (*taking Granfer's arm*) Only this one. (*She sings*)

2. Song (Molly, Granfer and Chorus)

During the song Molly dances with Granfer

After the number, the chorus exit R *and* L

Granfer is exhausted and Molly helps him to the table where he sits. While Molly has her back turned, helping the barmaids collect up tankards, he sneaks one and puts it to his lips. Molly turns and sees him

Granfer!

Startled Granfer spits out the ale, bangs down the tankard and gets to his feet

Granfer Oh rats! Oi be goin' down to the (*local pub*). They bain't so finicky!

Grumbling, he hobbles out down L

The barmaids exit into the inn as . . .

A group of children enter from up R. *One carries a large gift-wrapped box with a big bow of pink ribbon*

Molly Hello, children!

Children Hello, Miss Muffet!

1st Boy We've come to wish Dame Drinkup a happy birthday.

1st Girl (*pointing to the box*) And we've brought her a present.

Molly That's kind of you.

2nd Boy Is she in?

Molly Not at the moment. She's out shopping.

Children (*disappointed*) Oh!

Molly She should be back at any minute. Why don't you all come and wait at the inn. Then you can give it to her personally. (*She moves to the inn*)

1st Boy (*aside to the others with evil intent*) Oh, we'll give it to her, all right!

They snigger, move to the inn and exit with Molly

Dame (*off* R) Yoicks! Tally ho!

Two Fishermen enter from up R, *pushing a supermarket trolley. It is full of shopping and Dame Dolly Drinkup. They push her around the stage*

(*Yelling with delight*) Weeeee! Faster, boys! Faster! Next stop, Brands Hatch (*or local place*)! Tally Ho! Eat your heart out, Barry Sheene! Weeeee! Brrrum! Brrrum!

Eventually the Fishermen bring the trolley to a sudden halt and Dame Drinkup is thrown forward

(*To the audience*) Coo! Me whole life flashed before me! All nineteen years of it! (*To the fishermen*) Thanks Starsky! Thanks Hutch! Well! Don't just stand there like a couple of boiled owls, help a lady down, can't yer!

They lift her from the trolley and she pedals in mid-air

Weeee!

They put her down with a bump

What a let-down! I'm all up in a heap now! (*She adjusts her clothes*) That's better! Now, how much do I owe you boys for the taxi service?

1st fisherman Oh, that's all right, Dame Drinkup.

2nd fisherman Yes, it's our birthday present to you.

Dame Ta ever so kindly.

1st fisherman How old *are* you today?

Dame Oh, you forward fisherman, you! Don't you know it's rude to ask a young lady her age!

2nd fisherman He didn't ask a *young* lady, he asked *you*!

Dame (*to the audience*) What a sauce! (*To the fishermen*) If you must know, I'm (*she preens herself*) twenty-five.

They laugh

1st fisherman I asked how old you are not how many years you've been drawing old-age pension!

Dame Oh! You sarky so-and-so's! Get out of here before I forget I'm a lady and lay one on ya!

They exit down R, *laughing their heads off*

(*To the audience*) Hello everybody!

A few replies

(*Calling into the wings*) Oy! This lot have dozed off! (*To the audience*) What's the matter? Don't you know who I am! I am Dame Dolly Drinkup and I'm the landlady of yonder hostility. (*To a person in the front row*) That's boozer to you, dear! Now, listen. When I shout—"Hello everybody"—I want you all to shout back—"Hello Dame Drinkup!" Think you can do that? Good! Here goes—*hello everybody!*

The audience shout back

Lousy! Have another bash! Give yer tonsils a treat! *Hello everybody!*

The audience shout back

That's more like it! Well, what do you think of the show so far?

"*Rubbish*"

Yes, well, it'll be all right now cos *I'm* 'ere! And I'm not rubbish, am I?

"*Yes*"

Oh, no I'm not!

"*Oh, yes you are*" . . . *etc.*

Oh, you are a cheeky lot! Still, I'm used to it. What I've got to put up with in that pub! It'd make Bet Lynch hang up her ear-rings, it would really! I've tried to turn it into a second (*local posh pub or hotel*). I even got the barmaids to go topless! But that didn't work! It was just a great big *flop!* (*She goes to the trolley*) I've just been down to—(*local shop or supermarket*)—an' done me shoppin'. I 'ope I haven't squashed me perishables. Let's see! (*She takes out various items, first a bottle of Harpic*) This, 'cos I'm goin' clean round the bend! (*A toilet roll*) Writing paper! (*A packet of sweets*) Oh! Look! I've bought far too many sweets and as you can see I'm slimmin'. (*Coming forward*) Would you like some sweeties?

"*Yes*"

Say please then! Where was you brung up to! (*She throws packets out to the audience*) Here you are! Sweets for the sweets! Jellies for the bellies! Pops for the pops! Gums for the mums! Acid drops for the mothers-in-law! All gone! Now I'm goin' to sing to you! You'll like that, won't you?

"*Yes*" or "*No*"

What good taste you've got! (*Or*) Well, I'm goin' to, so there! (*To Conductor or Pianist*) Move it, Mozart!

3. Comedy Song (Dame)

To end, the Dame can dance with the trolley, pushing it off-stage down L *to finish*

Molly enters from the inn, followed by the children

Molly Hello, Aunty!
Dame Hello, Molly dear. (*She sees the children*) Oh, oh! I see you've got the Bash Street Kids with you!
Molly They've got something to say to you, Aunty.

The children sing "Happy Birthday" to Dame Drinkup

Dame (*overcome*) Oh! Bless their little cotton socks! (*Patting the first boy on the head; to the audience*) Aren't they little angels!
1st Boy How old are you?
Dame (*grabbing him around the throat*) And they're goin' the right way to get their wings!
1st Girl Please tell us how old you are, Dame Drinkup.
Children Yes!
Dame Shan't! You're as young as you feel and beauty is only skin deep!
2nd Boy Then you must be inside out!

The children laugh

Dame Oh! You rude little rotters! (*To the audience*) I don't know what kids are comin' to, do you? It's the parents I blame! (*To the children*) You ought to have had my dad! He'd have taught you a thing or two!
4th Boy Yes, how to build the *Ark* in six easy lessons!

The children laugh. The Dame takes the 4th boy by the ear

Dame Why don't you go and hire yourself out as a dartboard! (*She pushes* *the boy away*) Go on! Push off, the lot of you!

Molly Don't send them away, Aunty. The children have got something to give you.

Dame (*rolling up her sleeves*) Yes, and I'd like to give *them* something!

The children move to the Dame and hold out the box

Children Happy birthday, Dame Drinkup!

Dame (*all anger gone*) Oo! A prezzy for little me!? (*She takes the box*) And what a big one!

All the children back away from the Dame

(*Rattling the box near her ear*) I wonder what it can be.

4th Girl Why don't you open it and find out!

The children all snigger

1st Boy We hope your birthday goes with a *bang*, Dame Drinkup!

Children It will!

1st Girl (*to the Dame*) Go on! Open it!

Dame Before I do, I have an announcement to make. As you've been so kind, I'm going to take you for a picnic in the woods. My birthday treat! There! What do you think of that!

The children cheer, then suddenly become worried and get into a huddle. This is not seen by Dame Drinkup who has turned to Molly

(*To Molly*) We'll close the pub for the rest of the day. They can go to the (*local pub*) and get sloshed. Now! Let's see what the dear kiddie-winkies have given me! (*She starts to undo the ribbon*)

The huddle of children move forward

1st Boy If she opens that box, bang goes Dame Drinkup and bang goes the picnic!

3rd Girl What are we going to do?

2nd Girl We've got to stop her somehow!

1st Boy I've got an idea. Listen ...

They gather around him as he whispers his plan. Meanwhile Dame Drinkup is having difficulty undoing the ribbon

Dame Coo! It's done up tighter than Dolly Parton's stays! Isn't it excitin'. Just like Christmas all over again!

Suddenly the children rush over, join hands and dance around the Dame and Molly, singing "Happy Birthday". The 1st Boy snatches the box and runs downstage L with it. He throws it off-stage and rejoins the ring of children

Stop! Stop!

The children stop dancing around

Me prezzy! Where's me prezzy! Where is it?

There is a flash and loud explosion off-stage, down L. Granfer Fuddlewick staggers in from down L. He has lost his hat and his face is black. His smock is burnt and hanging in tatters, and if possible, still smouldering. Around his neck hangs the bow of ribbon from the box. He is dazed to say the least

Granfer Fuddlewick! (*Going to him*) Have you been at that cider again! I warned you ... (*she sees the ribbon*) Oy! That's the ribbon off my prezzy!

The children have started to creep towards down R exit

(*Turning*) Hold it, you lot! FREEZE!

The children freeze

Come 'ere!

They turn and move reluctantly to the Dame

(*Pointing to Granfer*) That was meant for me, wasn't it?
Children No!
Dame Oh yes, it was! I'm not as green as I'm cabbage lookin'. Well you can forget all about the picnic! It's off! You've burnt your boats good an' proper!
Granfer (*shaking one leg*) Tain't me *boats* oi be worried about!
Dame (*rounding on him*) Shut up, you ... you carbonized old clot, you!
Granfer (*to the audience*) What zomme folk'll do to stop a man havin' a drink!

He staggers off down L

Dame (*to the children*) Get out of my sight, the lot of you!
1st Boy We're sorry, Dame Drinkup!
1st Girl Please let us have the picnic!
Dame (*folded arms*) No!
Molly It was only a bit of fun, Aunty.
Dame Fun! A bit of fun, you call it! They could 'ave split me atom and shattered me illusions! I could have been deaded!
Molly Granfer's still alive.
Dame Don't make it worse!
Molly Please don't disappoint the children. Let them have the picnic.
Dame (*to the audience*) Shall I?
Audience Yes!
Dame Oh ... All right, then!
Children Hurrah!
Dame Only no more fireworks! Come on, Molly, let's go and pack the picnic hampster and get into our glad rags!

Dame and Molly exit into the inn

Children (*dancing for joy*) Hurrah! We're going on a picnic! We're going on a picnic! We're going on a picnic!

The beat of a drum and the clash of cymbals is heard off up R. The children stop and listen

1st Boy Hey! Listen! What's that?
1st Girl I don't know, but it's coming this way!

The chorus enter from all directions and group themselves around the stage.

The barmaids enter from the inn. From up R, *Jasper Grasper enters, grandly waving his top hat. He is closely followed by Flop, beating a big drum and Flip clashing a pair of cymbals. They parade around the stage, then Flop trips and falls on his back with the drum on top of him. He kicks his legs and yells, unable to get up. Flip goes to his rescue and they get into a hopeless tangle. The crowd roar with laughter. Grasper, enraged, pulls the two clowns apart, and drags them downstage*

Grasper (*aside to them*) You blithering blockheads! How dare you show me up in front of these perishing peasants! Get out and prepare for the dance! Get out! (*He pushes them towards* R)

Flip and Flop, with drum and cymbals, scuttle out up R

Grasper turns to the crowd and addresses them in his best theatrical voice and manner

(*To the crowd*) Ladies and gentlemen—(*to the audience, with a sneer*)—and others! (*Back to the crowd*) Allow me to introduce myself. I am the Great Jasper Grasper! Showman extraordinaire. Good people of Periwinkle, prepare to feast your eyes on two of the finest performers ever to set foot outside (*local place*). (*He gestures flamboyantly towards* R *with his top hat*) Behold! I give you the fantastic, the fabulous—Flip and Flop!

A fanfare or roll on drums. Everyone looks R. *Nothing happens*

(*With a grimace, louder*) The fabulous Flip and Flop!

Another fanfare or roll on drums. Everyone looks R *again, but still nothing happens. Grasper goes to* R *and snarls off-stage*

GET IN HERE, YOU DOZY DUNDERHEADS! (*He returns to* C *and gestures with his hat as before*) Behold! The fabulous Flip and Flop!

Yet another fanfare or roll on drums. Everyone looks R

Flip and Flop appear very sheepishly and join Grasper C. *They both wear fezzes and old fashioned night-shirts. There are worn over their troubadour costumes. Flip's shirt is very short and Flop's very long so he keeps tripping up*

(*To the crowd*) And now! Flip and Flop will perform, especially for you, a dance from the exotic expanses of Egypt! (*With a flourish*) The Sand Dance!

Sand Dance music starts but Flip and Flop don't

(*Pushing them forward*) Get on with it! (*To the crowd with a flourish*) The Sand Dance!

4. Sand Dance (Flip and Flop)

Flip and Flop perform the Sand Dance and make a complete comic mess of it. The crowd groan and some even boo and hiss. Grasper goes round with his hat held out for a collection

Gruff Fisherman Pay for *that*! You must be jokin'!
Villagers Rubbish! Lousy!, *etc.*

Little Girl (*to Grasper*) Don't ring us, we'll ring you!

The chorus and children exit R *and* L

Grasper You blithering buffoons! You blundering blockheads!

Flip (*to the audience*) I don't think he likes us!

Grasper Try to make a fool out of me, would you!

Flop No, you're doin' a good job of that on your own!

Grasper Ahh! I'm warning the pair of you! If your act doesn't improve, you're *out*! (*Moving away from them, dramatically*) Oh! To think that I, the Great Jasper Grasper, should be reduced to this! (*Hand on his chest*) I, who once played Hamlet for GIELGUD!

Flop (*copying Grasper's style*) And I, who once played centre-forward for (*local football team*).

Grasper (*rounding on them again*) Bah! I will give you *one* hour to improve your act, or *out you go*! Then you will have to go back to Crossroads (*or other TV soap opera*)!

Flip } (*begging on their knees*) Oh no! Anything but that!
Flop }

Grasper One hour to improve! Get rehearsing! (*Pointing to the audience*) And don't let these miserable peasants interrupt you!

Flop Oh, they won't do that! (*To the audience*) Will you?

Audience No!

Grasper They'd better not, or I'll go down there and sort 'em out!

After a little by-play with the audience, Grasper exits down L

As soon as he is out of sight, Flop runs over and blows a loud raspberry after him

Flip I don't think he heard that!

Flop Let's make sure he does. (*To the audience*) Come on, you lot! Let's all give old Grasper a real big, juicy raspberry! After three! One—two—three!

Flip, Flop and the audience blow a raspberry

Grasper, snarling, runs back on, shakes his fist at the audience and exits

(*To the audience, squirming with delight*) Cor! That was good!

Flip Come on. I suppose we'd better start rehearsing or old Grumpy Guts'll give us the push.

Flop Oh, I'm fed up with that old Sand Dance! Let's do our song instead.

Flip Good idea! You start.

Flop does a short send up of a "pop" song. He sustains a wailing high note

Dame Drinkup enters from the inn. She is dressed for the picnic in a frilly dress and outrageous hat

Dame (*as she enters*) Where's the fire! (*She sees Flip and Flop and moves down to them. She peers into Flop's open mouth*)

He becomes aware of her and stops his wail

Where is it?

Flop Where's what?

Dame The pain?

Flip He's not in pain. He's singing!

Dame *Singin'!* Ha! you call that *singin'*! It sounded like (*pop singer*) with his tonsils toasted! Push off the pair of you!

Flip Oh, don't be hard on us. You've got a kind face.

Flop Yeah, we don't know *what* kind, but you've got one!

Flip We haven't eaten for two whole days!

Dame You won't get a bite out of me!

Flop (*to the audience*) Who'd want one! Yuck!

Dame You'll never make a livin' with '*im* singin'. And believe me, I know! *I'm* a singist! A good one! (*Pointing to the audience*) Ask them! Why, if I'd wanted to, I could have been a second Shirley Bassey!

Flop (*to the audience*) Looks more like a second Shirley Williams!

Dame (*singing*) TRA LA LA! I could have been great in opera! Oh, I would have been a knock-out singin' Carmen!

Flop We know that one!

Flip }
Flop } (*singing*)   Carmen to the garden, Maud ...

Dame How dare you make fun of me! I've never been so insulted in all my life!

Flip Oh, come on! With a face like that you must have been!

She chases Flip and Flop off down R. *The children and chorus enter from all directions. Granfer Fuddlewick, now cleaned up, is with them. Everyone is chattering excitedly about something. The children run straight to Dame Drinkup*

Children Dame Drinkup! Dame Drinkup!

1st Boy You'll never guess who's here!

Dame Russell Harty (*or popular local or TV personality*)?

1st Girl No! It's Captain Jack Dauntless!

Dame (*over the moon*) Oh, CAPTAIN JACK DAUNTLESS! Oh, my! (*She preens herself*)

Molly enters from the inn. She is prettily dressed for the picnic. The barmaids follow her

Molly (*going to the Dame*) What's all the excitement about, Aunty?

Dame Captain Jack Dauntless is here!

Molly (*puzzled*) Who is Captain Jack Dauntless?

Dame (*in disbelief*) *Who* is CAPTAIN JACK DAUNTLESS!! Surely you've heard of him, dear! He's made a big splash in seafaring circles! He's sailed around the world so many times, he doesn't know his aft from his Benbow! He's explored more foreign parts than Dr (*local doctor*) and he's ever so handsome!

Molly He sounds fascinating. I should like to meet him.

Dame Well, now's yer chance, girl! Here he comes!

The crowd cheer as ...

Handsome Jack Dauntless enters at the back on the raised walk. He is followed by sailors. Jack pauses and salutes

Jack (*to the crowd*) Ahoy there!
All (*saluting back*) Ahoy Cap'n!

Jack comes down the steps and sings

5. Song (Jack and chorus)

If desired a dance by Jack, sailors and barmaids can follow the song

Dame (*gushing*) Welcome to Periwinkle-on-Sea, Captain. I'm Dame Dolly
Drinkup and I own ponder yub ... I mean, yonder pub!
Jack Top'o the morning to you!
Dame And the top'o the milk to *you*! This is my niece, Little Miss Molly
Muffet.

*Jack turns and sees Molly for the first time. It is obviously love at first sight
between them*

Jack (*holding out his hand*) How do you do, Miss Muffet.
Molly (*taking his hand*) I'm very pleased to meet you, Captain Dauntless.
Jack (*keeping hold of her hand*) Please call me Jack.
Molly (*shyly*) Jack.

They gaze into each other's eyes

Dame (*playing up to Jack*) Today's my birthday, Captain.
Jack Why, shiver me timbers and rumple me riggin'! Many happy returns
of the day!

He slaps her heartily on the back and she almost falls over

Dame (*recovering*) Er ... th ... thank you! Yes, it's me birthday and I've
decided to take everyone for a picnic in the forest—(*with a flamboyant
gesture*)—to *celebrate*!
Jack What a splendid gesture!
Dame Oh, did you like it? I'll do it again! (*She repeats the flamboyant
gesture*)
Jack (*laughing*) No, I meant it's a splendid gesture taking everyone on a
picnic.
Dame Oh, well, that's me. I've always had a big heart!
Granfer You've always 'ad a big *everything*, Dolly Drinkup! Hee! Hee! Hee!
Dame *Push off*, you prehistoric Peter Pan! (*Sweetly to Jack*) I was wonderin'
if you'd care to come along for a nibble, Captain?
Jack Well ... er ... it's very nice of you to ask me, but I'm afraid I have lots
to attend to while I'm in port, so——
Molly It would be an honour to have you accompany us, Captain ... er ...
Jack.
Jack Are *you* going on the picnic?
Molly Yes.
Jack Well, in that case, my duties can wait. Yes, Dame Drinkup, I'd be
delighted to join your picnic.
Dame Oh! Goody goody gum drops!
Granfer Can oi come?
Dame No!
Granfer Oh, go on! (*To the crowd*) Tell 'er to let oi come!

Children Let him come! *Please!* Go on, Dame Drinkup ... *etc., etc.*
Dame Oh! ... All right!
Granfer (*dancing for joy*) YIPEEEEE!! (*He kisses the Dame on her cheek*)

Everyone laughs

> *Dame Drinkup takes a swing at him, misses and exits into the inn*

> *Jack and Molly exit* UR, *arm in arm. The crowd follow them off*

Granfer is about to follow, when ...

> *The Dame appears at the inn door*

Dame (*calling to Granfer*) Oy! RAMBO! I've got something for you!
Granfer (*scuttling across, rubbing his hands*) Be it a bottle o' beer?
Dame No, it's this 'ere!

She pulls a large picnic hamper from the inn and dumps it on Granfer. His legs buckle under its weight. The Dame pushes him to C

> MUSH! MUSH! (*She pushes him towards* R) MUSH! MUSH! (*To the audience*) See you at the picnic!

> *She waves to the audience and makes a comedy exit with Granfer as ...*

The Lights fade to Black-out

SCENE 2

A Street in Periwinkle

Tabs, or a frontcloth showing quaint cottages with the sea beyond

Flip and Flop enter. Flop is eating sweets from a large paper bag. They are back in their troubadour costumes

Flip Why did you have to buy all those sweets?
Flop (*mouth full*) Mmm! Mmmm! (*Offering the bag*) Mmm?
Flip No, thanks. I'm sweet enough!

Flop chokes with laughter. Flip thumps him on the back

Flop (*gulping down a sweet*) Cor! That one went down so fast, it knocked me tonsils inside out! Now, I'll have to have another one! (*He takes a sweet and starts chewing*)
Flip If you eat any more your teeth'll fall out!
Flop (*shaking his head*) Mmm!
Flip What do you mean—(*he copies Flop*)—"Mmm!"

Flop takes from the bag a set of "clicking teeth". He chases Flip with them

> (*Turning away*) Put 'em away! Put those horrible things away!

Flop grabs at Flip's bottom with the clicking teeth. Comic business

> You're a fool! What are you?
Flop A foooooool!

Flip You're two steps away from an idiot!

Flop I'll move then! (*He moves. He takes another sweet and chews it*)

Flip Stop eating those sweets! They're bad for you! I bet the boys and girls don't eat sweets all the time.

Flop I bet they'd have one of *these* if I offered 'em one! (*To the audience*) Hands up all those who want a sweetie! (*After counting the hands*) There, Mr Know-All-Knickers!

Flip Well, go on then.

Flop Go on what?

Flip Give 'em your sweets!

Flop But I won't have any left!

Flip Well, you should have thought of that before you opened yer big cake'ole!

Flop (*to the audience*) You don't want my nasty, sticky sweets, do you?

Audience YES!

Flop Oh, no you don't!

Audience Oh yes, we do!

Flip (*to Flop*) If you don't hand 'em out they'll come up here and take 'em!

Flop No, they won't! They're too scared!

Flip We'll see about that! (*To the audience*) Who'd like to come up? Let's have some of you up here! This way! Come on down!

The House Lights go up and some children from the audience come up onstage. Flip arranges them in a line and asks their names, etc.

(*To Flop*) Right then, start dishin' out!

Flop gives the children his sweets (small packets of sweets and chocolate bars). Flip gets the audience to applaud the children then helps them off the stage. The House Lights fade out. Flop looks in his bag, finds it empty and starts wailing

Flop (*wailing*) It's empty!

Flip Serves you right! Hey! We'd better not hang about or old Grasper'll have our guts for garters! (*To the audience*) If you see him give us a shout.

Jasper Grasper enters and moves behind them

The audience start shouting "He's behind you!" Flip and Flop turn slowly. Grasper turns at the same time, keeping behind them. "Oh, no he isn't", "Oh, yes he is" routine. Eventually Jasper plants his hands on their shoulders. They react in horror

Flip Ahh! It's Dirty Den (*or popular TV villain*)!!

Grasper Bah! You lazy loafers! I can't take me eyes off you for a single minute!

Flop (*smoothing his eyebrows*) Oh! I didn't know you cared!

Grasper I told you to rehearse your act!

Flip Well, he ... I ... we ... they ... we can't rehearse in the street, can we?

Flop No, people'd think we was daft!

Grasper You *are* daft! Listen! There is a forest nearby. Go and rehearse there! Go On! *Move!*

They run off-stage

(*To the audience*) If only I could find a decent act! Then I could ditch those two nincompoops for ever! You know what I need, don't you?

The audience tells him

And the same to you, with knobs on! What I need is a big draw! Something that will draw big crowds!

Flip appears from the wings

Flip We've got something that will draw big crowds!

Flop appears on the other side, holding a six-foot pencil

A BIG PENCIL!
Grasper Get out, imbeciles!

Grasper chases them off, as . . .

The Lights fade to Black-out

SCENE 3

A Glade in the Forest

There are tall trees on both sides. In one tree there is a huge cobweb. The backcloth shows more of the forest with a distant view of Periwinkle and the sea. The picnic hamper is set LC

Some of the chorus are discovered dancing a rustic dance. The others are grouped around watching the dance and clapping in time to the music. Granfer and the children are seated on the ground near the hamper. Dame Drinkup, fast asleep, is sitting on the hamper

6. Rustic Dance (Chorus)

After the dance, the chorus saunter off each side

Dame Drinkup snores loudly. Granfer and the children get up and gather round her. Granfer takes a large paper bag from his pocket. He blows it up and bangs it near the Dame's ear. She wakes with a yell and rolls off the hamper

Dame (*rolling on the ground*) Help! Oo! I've been shot! I've been shot! (*She sits up and searches for bullet holes*) Call a doctor! Call the RSPCA! I've been—— (*She sees the bag in Granfer's hand and leaps to her feet*) It was you, you horrible old hooligan! How dare you! I was 'avin' a lovely dream too! This handsome Arab sheik rode up, threw me across his saddle, and carried me off into the desert!
Granfer (*to the children*) Coo! Oi bet that buckled 'is mudguards! Hee! Hee! Hee!

The children laugh

Dame Hey! Where's Captain Dauntless and Molly?
1st Boy They went for a walk in the forest.
1st Girl Yes, a nature ramble!

The children and Granfer giggle

Dame I expect Molly's showin' him the beauty spots.
Granfer Oi bet she is! Cor! Hee! Hee! Hee!
Dame That's enough of that, you rude old reprobate!
2nd Boy Can we play some games now, Dame Drinkup?
Dame What's it to be? Something nice and quiet, like I spy or——
Granfer *(together)* Blindman's Buff!
Children
Dame *(to the audience, glumly)* Blindman's Buff! I might have known! (*To the children*) And who's goin' to be blindfolded? As if I didn't know!
Granfer *(together)* You!
Children
Dame *(to the audience)* What a flippin' surprise!

They blindfold her and spin her around a couple of times. This done, Granfer and the children creep off-stage, leaving the Dame feeling about with arms outstretched. Eventually she fumbles her way off-stage, L

Molly enters from up R, closely followed by Jack who looks at her adoringly. She keeps her back to him

Molly *(meaning the forest)* It's very beautiful, isn't it?
Jack *(meaning her)* Oh, yes!
Molly And particularly pretty at this time of year.
Jack At *any* time of the year, I should think!
Molly *(turning to face him)* I'm so glad you like our forest.
Jack *(gazing at her, dreamily)* Forest? What about the forest?
Molly *(smiling)* I've been talking about it for the last five minutes.
Jack What!? (*He comes down to earth*) Oh! Yes!
Molly *(looking about)* Oh, dear!
Jack What's wrong?
Molly Where's Aunty and the children?
Jack The hamper's still here. Perhaps she took them for a walk.

Molly busies herself at the hamper and Jack comes forward to speak to the audience

Now the coast is clear, I'm going to tell her how much I love her. It ought to be plain sailing. Wish me luck, shipmates! (*He adjusts his hat, tugs his uniform and turns to Molly*) Er ... Molly?
Molly *(coming down)* Yes?
Jack Up until today, my ship the *Pretty Polly* was the only girl I've ever cared for. But now that I've met you, I ... I ... (*He turns away, annoyed at himself*) Oh, blisterin' barnacles!
Molly *(moving to him)* Jack, what are you trying to say?
Jack *(turning and taking her hands)* Oh, Molly! Molly darling! This is what I'm trying to say! (*He sings*)

7. Duet (Jack and Molly)

After the duet, they kiss and Molly moves away, shyly

Molly *(for want of something to say)* I ... I hope Aunt Dolly and the children aren't lost.

Jack Don't worry your pretty little head. You wait here. I'll go and find 'em!

He exits down R.

Molly hugs herself with joy and dances on the spot, humming the refrain from the duet. She sits on the hamper and gazes dreamily out front

From behind a tree up R, *the Spider appears. It sees Molly and creeps slowly towards her. The audience will be shouting "Behind you", "Look behind you", etc.*

Molly (*rising and moving forward, to the audience*) What's the matter? What is it? Behind me? What's behind me? (*She turns and sees the Spider. She screams and runs to down* L)

HELP! JACK! HELP ME! HELP!

Jack runs on from up R *with drawn sword. He rushes across and plants himself between Molly and the Spider*

Jack (*jabbing at the Spider with his sword*) Back, you brute! Back I say!

The Spider backs away. It trembles with fright, trips and falls to the ground. Jack towers over it with his sword ready to strike

Spider (*terrified*) NO! *Please!* Please don't kill me! I wasn't going to hurt her! Please don't kill me! Please!

Jack and Molly are dumbstruck

Jack A . . . a talking spider! I . . . I don't believe it. I must be dreaming!
Molly (*moving to him*) You're not. I heard it too.

They move a little nearer to the Spider. It starts to cry pitifully

It's . . . it's crying! (*She moves to the Spider and kneels beside it. Softly to the Spider*) Please . . . please, don't cry. (*She puts a tentative hand on the Spider*) It's all right. No-one is going to hurt you.

The Spider looks up at Molly and its crying subsides. It gets to its feet, helped by Molly. Jack puts his sword away

Spider I . . . I'm very sorry if I frightened you. I didn't mean to.
Molly I can see that now. But you did give me rather a shock. You're very large for a spider.
Spider Yes! I know! But, you see . . . I'm not really a spider at all.

Jack and Molly exchange puzzled glances

I'll explain. I am Princess Valtina of Valador. My father and mother are King Valentine and Queen Valtora. See! I carry the Royal Crest of Valador. (*She holds out a small medallion that hangs from a chain around her neck*)

Jack and Molly peer at it

Jack (*aghast*) Why, shiver me timbers! (*He bows low*) *Your highness!*
Molly (*with a curtsy*) Your highness! This is Captain Jack Dauntless and I am Molly Muffet.

Spider I am pleased to make your acquaintance.

Jack If it's not a rude question, Princess, how did you become a spider?

Spider I will tell you. It all began a year ago. Valador was a beautiful, peaceful paradise. Everyone living there was happy and carefree. *Then*—a dark shadow fell upon our land. MORAC came!

Jack ⎱ (*together*) MORAC?
Molly ⎰

Spider YES! An evil witch. She decided to live in Valador and reduce all its loveliness to desolation. One night she came to the Royal Palace and took us all prisoner! I picked up the Royal Teapot and threw it at her. She was so angry she cast the most awful spell on me and I turned into what you see now ... (*She starts to cry*) A huge ... (*sniff*) ... ugly ... (*sniff*) ... SPIDER! (*She cries pitifully*)

Molly (*putting her arm around the Spider*) Please don't cry, your highness. (*To Jack*) I wish there was something we could do to help!

Jack Princess, how did you get *here*?

Spider (*after a loud sniff*) After Morac had cast her spell, I ran away as fast as my eight legs would carry me! I ran and ran! I crossed mountains, rivers and seas before I found myself in this forest. I've been hiding here for months, afraid to show myself. I knew people would be frightened or laugh at me!

Molly Well, you're amongst friends now.

Spider Oh, I'm so glad I've found someone to talk to after all this time. But I'm so worried about my poor mother and father. Who knows what Morac might have done to them.

Jack Your highness, my ship and its crew are at your service. We'll sail for Valador, find your parents and spike Morac's guns into the bargain.

Spider (*delighted*) You *will*! (*Taking their hands*) Oh, thank you! Thank you! Thank you!

Granfer, children and the chorus enter from R and L. They are all talking and laughing amongst themselves. One of the sailors sees the spider

Sailor (*calling to the others and pointing*) HEY! LOOK! LOOK!

They all go silent and gape at the strange creature

Female villager What *is* it?

Fisherman It's a giant spider!

Granfer (*to a female villager*) Fancy 'avin' one that size in yer bath, missis!

The female screams and hides her face

Spider (*very frightened and clinging to Molly*) Please don't let them hurt me!

The crowd are awestruck

Male villager Did you hear that!

Sailor It can *talk*!

Children A talking spider!

There is uproar from the crowd

Jack (*bringing them to order*) BELAY! SILENCE!

The uproar dies down

Have some respect! You are in the presence of royalty. (*Bringing the
Spider forward*) This is Princess Valtina of Valador!
Granfer A talkin' spider! Oi be proper in need of a drink *now*!
Dame (*off* L) Yoo hoo! Here I come! I'm comin' to get you!

Dame Drinkup enters down L. *She is still blindfolded and feeling her way
about. The crowd keep clear of her as she fumbles to* C

I'll catch one of you in a minute! I know you're 'ere! You just wait . . . (*She
touches and grabs the Spider*) Got yer! I win! Now, which of you little
scamps is it?
Molly Aunty——
Dame No! Don't tell me! Let me guess! (*She feels the Spider's head*) Mm!
Hairy! Well, it's not Old Granfer Fuddlewick, unless he's had a trans-
plant! Now let's see who I've caught! (*She reaches for the blindfold*)
Granfer (*aside to the children, rubbing his hands in glee*) Hee! Hee! This
ought to be good, kids!
Dame (*pulling off the blindfold*) THERE! Now, let me—— (*She looks at the
Spider. She does a double-take, screams and runs down* L) AHHH! HELP!
GREAT HAIRY HORRORS! Call a doctor! I'm seeing things. I'm
havin' ILLUMINATIONS! I . . . I thought I saw a (*she gulps*)—GIANT
SPIDER!
Molly You did! (*Pointing to the Spider*) Look!

The Dame looks, blinks her eyes and looks again

Dame (*to the audience*) WELL! I'll go to the foot of our compost heap! (*In
sudden fright*) Ahh! It's real! It's real! Oh, keep it away from me! (*Business
with holding skirts up*)
Jack Calm down, Dame Drinkup. There's nothing to be frightened of. This
is Princess Valtina of Valador.
Dame I don't care if it's Spiderman's Granny, don't let it come near me!
Jack To cut a long story short, Princess Valtina was turned into a spider by
a wicked witch.
Dame Oh, give over, Captain! You've been watchin' too much Jackanory!
Spider (*moving a little nearer to the Dame*) He is telling you the truth.
Dame Well, I still don't—— (*Double-take*) Ah! It can *talk*! A talkin' spider!
(*To the audience*) I'm goin' BONKERS!

Flip and Flop enter at the back and stand watching

Molly (*to the Spider*) This is my aunt, Dame Drinkup.
Spider (*holding out a leg to the Dame*) I'm very pleased to make your
acquaintance.
Dame (*gingerly taking the Spider's leg*) Charmed to meet you, your royal
lowness. Ta ever so! (*She makes an awkward curtsy*)
Molly (*to the Dame*) Jack intends sailing to Valador and helping Princess
Valtina's parents. In the meantime can she stay with us at the *Fillet Inn*?
Dame (*doubtfully*) Well, I don't know . . . (*To Spider*) Would you like to
stay with me, Princess?
Spider Oh, yes please! You're very kind, Dame Drinkup.
Dame Oh, charmed ever so kindly, thank you very much! Perhaps, you'd
like to help me in the bar on Saturday night. I could use an extra pair of

hands, and hands, and hands, and ... Oh, come on! Let's go home!

To suitable music, Dame Drinkup and Molly take the Spider's legs ,and dance her around. They then exit with her L. Jack, Granfer and the others follow. Two of the men carry off the picnic hamper. As soon as they have all gone, Flip and Flop make a comic exit on the other side as ...

The Lights fade to Black-out

SCENE 4

The Street again

Tabs, or the frontcloth used in Scene 2

Jasper Grasper enters from R and walks across. Halfway he spots the audience and stops to give them a snarl. They respond with boos and hisses

Grasper BAH! You miserable mob of (*local place*) MORONS! *What* are you? How dare you answer me back! Any more of that and I'll come down there and crush yer crisps and pulverize yer Polos! BAH! Where are those two dunderheads! It's time we moved on to another town! This one stinks!

The audience reacts

Ah! I've had enough of you!

He exits L, amid boos and hisses

Flip and Flop enter from R

Flip (*to the audience*) Cor! What did you think of that, folks! A talking spider!
Flop (*to the audience*) Ugh! I don't like creepy crawly spiders! Do you?
Audience Yes! (*or*) No!
Flip But this one's special! It can *talk*!
Flop I don't care if it sings with (*pop group*), I didn't like it! I've never seen anything so 'orrible!

Jasper Grasper enters from L

Grasper Ah!
Flop (*to the audience*) CORRECTION!
Grasper WELL! Have you been rehearsing your act?!
Flip Well, Boss, we went to the forest like you said, and we were just about to start, when we saw a spider.
Grasper (*advancing on them, threateningly*) YOU!!!
Flip NO BOSS, WAIT! It wasn't just any old spider. It was about this big ... (*he indicates the Spider's size*)
Grasper PAH!
Flop And it can TALK!
Grasper YOU KNUCKLEHEADS! Do you expect me to believe a story like that!

Flop It's true! (*He points to the audience*) They saw it as well! (*To the audience*) Didn't you?

Audience YES!

Grasper (*sneering at the audience*) Well, they're just as stupid as you are! Very well, my fine fellows! Where is it? Show me this enormous talking spider! (*Aside*) Ha! That's called their bluff!

Flip Dame Drinkup took it home with her.

Grasper Ha! A likely story!

Flop (*looking off* L) Here she comes now! You can ask her yourself.

Dame Drinkup enters from L, *followed by Granfer. She carries a shopping bag filled with rolls of gaudy wallpaper*

Dame (*turning to Granfer as they enter*) Come on, Flash Gordon, make yourself useful! Carry the bag!

Granfer goes to pick her up. She hits him with a roll of paper

Not ME, you dozy old duffer! I said the BAG! I'm not a bag, am I?

Granfer is about to say something but she threatens him with a roll of paper

DON'T YOU DARE! DON'T YOU DARE!

She thrusts the bag at Granfer and turns to go but Grasper is standing in front of her. She pulls up short, reacts and looks at the Audience

(*In a loud whisper to the audience*) What's (*pop or TV star*) doin' 'ere?

Grasper (*to the Dame, removing his hat*) Do I have the pleasure——

Dame Not with me, you don't!

Grasper —of meeting Dame Drinkup?

Dame That's me!

Grasper Is it true that you have a . . . a special guest staying at your inn?

Dame Yes. It's Princess Valtina of Valador!

Grasper (*roaring with laughter*) Ha! Ha! Ha! Ha!

Dame (*to Flip and Flop*) What's the matter with him?

Flip He's laughing.

Dame Is that all! I thought he was goin' to lay an egg!

Grasper Ha! Ha! These two nitwits told me you had a talking spider staying with you! Ha! Ha! Ha! Ha! Ha!

Dame Well, don't do yerself a mischief! It's true!

Grasper gulps and chokes

Grasper (*with a wheeze*) True?!

Dame Yes, she was turned into a spider by a nasty old witch. But she can still talk, bless her little heart.

Suddenly, the stage goes dark except for an eerie green spotlight on Grasper. The others freeze

Grasper (*to the audience, melodramatically*) GAD! A talking spider! Just think what an attraction that would be! Jasper Grasper and his Talking Spider! Oh, I can hear the money rolling in now! (*Rubbing his hands*) Ha! Ha! Ha! I must have that spider! It shall be mine! All mine! But how? How? Ah! I have a plan!

The Lighting returns to normal. The others move again as if nothing has happened

(*To the Dame, very oily*) My dear Dame Drinkup, am I to understand that today is your birthday?

Dame YEP! All day!

Grasper Many happy returns! On such an auspicious day, I should like to place myself at your disposal. (*Moving close and leering*) Is there anything I can do for you?

Dame (*coyly*) Oh, you saucy so-and-so, you!

Granfer It would please me greatly to help such a sweet, attractive, charming, little creature. What can I do?

Grasper Get yer eyes tested! Hee! Hee! Hee!

Dame (*sidling up to Grasper*) Do you know something, if you were fifty years younger you could sweep me off my feet.

Granfer He'd 'ave to drive a bulldozer! Hee! Hee! Hee!

Dame I'll bulldoze *you* in a minute!

Grasper Aren't there any little jobs I can do for you around the house?

Dame No, I've got a little doggie that does them! No, I ... Oh, wait! I'm goin' to wallpaper me parlour. I've just been down to (*local decorating shop or DIY centre*) and bought me paper. You can give me a hand with that, if you like.

Grasper (*aside*) Ha! Ha! The very thing! (*To the Dame*) It will be a pleasure. (*Indicating Flip and Flop*) These two fine lads would be delighted to help you. (*To Flip and Flop*) Wouldn't you, boys? (*To the Dame quickly*) Yes, they would!

Dame Ta very muchly. (*To Flip and Flop*) Be at the *Fillet Inn* in ten minutes. (*To Granfer*) Come on, Fido! WALKIES!

She walks across to exit R, *and Granfer trots behind her. He stops and eyes Grasper suspiciously*

(*To Granfer*) Oh, what's up now?

Granfer (*eyeing Grasper*) Oi' smells a rat!

Dame This is no time to discuss your family! Get out!

She pushes him out in front of her and exits

Grasper (*pulling Flip and Flop forward*) Listen to me! Go to the inn and help the old trout with her wallpapering. As soon as the coast is clear, find that talking spider and bring it to the harbour! I'll be waiting there with a fast ship ready to sail!

Flop Why?

Grasper Don't ask questions, just do as I say! GO! GO!

They run out, R

(*To the audience*) Ha! Ha! Ha! Once I get my hands on that talking spider I'll make millions! MILLIONS! HA! HA! HA! I shall be able to buy a house in (*local posh area*). (*He starts singing*) "Money is the root of all evil, Money is the root of all evil, give it to me! Give it to me! Give it to *me*!" HA! HA! HA!

He dances off L, *amid boos and hisses as*

The Lights fade to Black-out

SCENE 5

Dame Drinkup's Parlour

The backcloth shows a fireplace with a crazy portrait of Dame Drinkup hanging over it, a dresser with cracked china, some patched furniture and a pile of beer barrels. The side wings are used for the slap-stick scene and must be firmly braced. At the back is a pasting table surrounded by paste buckets, rolls of wallpaper, brushes, a step-ladder, etc. There are entrances above and below the side wings

Molly, Jack and the Spider are discovered

Molly (*to the Spider*) And this is the parlour. It's in a bit of a mess I'm afraid. Aunty's just about to start wallpapering.
Spider It doesn't matter a bit. Oh, it's so nice to have a roof over my head again!

Dame Drinkup enters from down L. *She is dressed for wallpapering in a comic, fluorescent overall*

Dame Hello, your royalness! Well, what do you think of me 'umble 'ome?
Spider It's very nice.
Dame It's not a bad little dump, is it. I call it the South Fork of Periwinkle.
Spider Why?
Dame 'Cos you have to be *well-oiled* to live 'ere! It'll be real swish when I've had the improvements done! I'm goin' to 'ave me front double-glazed and one of them nice little glass *conservatives* built on at the back. That's if I can get the *labour* on *liberal* terms. Oh, it'll be like the *Queen Vic* when it's finished!
Spider I like it just the way it is. I can't thank you enough for all the kindness you've shown me.
Jack That's what friendship is all about!

8. Song and Dance (Jack, Molly, Dame and Spider)

This should be a comedy number with a dance routine. At first the Spider finds it difficult negotiating with her legs, but with the others' help, she soon gets the hang of it

After the number, Jack and Molly exit R

Dame (*to the Spider*) You must be worn out! Wouldn't you like to go to your room and put your legs up? There's a nice big cobweb in the corner that's vacant at the moment.
Spider (*moving to* L) Thank you, but I prefer the bed.

The Spider exits down L

Dame (*to the audience*) There's no flies on 'er! (*Rubbing her hands*) Now then! Let's get on with this paper hangin'. Where are those two Charlies?

Flip and Flop enter from down R. *They wear baggy comic overalls and enormous cloth caps*

(*Laughing*) Ha! Ha! Look! It's the little performations! Right, then, you two! Let's get stuck in!

A slap-stick paper-hanging scene follows. See Production Notes. Afterwards . . .

We've run out of paste! I'll have to go and make some more. Stick around, boys! Ha! Ha! *Stick* around! Get it? *Paste—stick around*—Oh, please yourself!

She exits up L *with a bucket*

Flip brings Flop downstage

Flip Now's our chance to get the Spider. It must be upstairs. (*He points down* L)

Flop (*frightened*) G-Go on, then!

Flip (*pushing him over*) You lead the way!

Flop I-I can't I-I've got a bone in my leg! (*Pushing Flip over*) You go!

Flip *Right!* I will! (*He marches down* L, *then stops*) Why *should* we! Why should we help Old Grasper! As soon as he gets that talking spider, he'll give *us* the sack! Let him do his own dirty work! Let's clear off! Let's leave the Old Grumble Guts for good!

Flop Yeah!

They run to exit down R, *but are stopped by the sudden appearance of Grasper*

Grasper So!

He advances on them and they back away from him

(*As he walks*) Where is it? Where's my talking spider? Where is it? Answer me!

Flip It's . . . it's upstairs! (*He points down* L)

Grasper Then what are you waiting for! Lead me to it! The ship is ready to sail! Make haste! Make haste!

He pushes them off down L *and exits*

Dame Drinkup enters from up L *with a full bucket of "paste"*

Dame (*as she enters*) Here we are! More lovely paste! Now, we can—— (*She sees she is alone. To the audience*) Look at that! *Typical!* As soon as me back's turned they've downed tools and walked out! Oh, that Arthur Scargill's got a lot to answer for!

Spider (*off* L, *screaming*) HELP! LET ME GO! HELP!

Dame (*coming down with the bucket*) What was that?!

Grasper strides on from down L. *Flip and Flop follow, dragging the struggling Spider between them*

Spider Dame Drinkup! HELP ME!

Dame (*to Grasper*) 'Ere! What do you think you're doin'!

Grasper OUT OF MY WAY!!

He grabs the bucket and dumps it on the Dame's head. She blunders about trying to get if off

(*To the audience*) HA! HA! No-one can stop *me*! (*To Flip and Flop*) Come, fools! Make haste! To the ship!

He runs out down R, *followed by Flip and Flop dragging the Spider*

Spider (*as she goes*) HELP! SAVE ME!

Dame Drinkup manages to pull the bucket from her head and throws it away. Comic business as she wipes the "paste" from her eyes and mouth

Dame (*to the audience*) Where's the Princess? Did he carry her off?
Audience YES!
Dame Oh, no! (*In a panic she runs up and down, yelling*) HELP! HELP! MURDER! KIDNAP! HELP! HELP! Ooo! (*She slips on some paste and falls over*)

Jack and Molly rush on from down R, *followed by the children. The chorus rush on from all other entrances and fill the stage*

Crowd What happened! What's wrong! What is it? . . . *etc.*

They help the Dame up

Molly *Aunty!* What happened?
Dame It was Jasper Grasper and his two men! They've kidnapped the Princess! They've VIADUCTED HER!

General panic

Granfer Fuddlewick scuttles on from down R

Granfer (*gasping*) Oi . . . oi . . . oi've just seen that Jasper Grasper sailin' off. 'E's got the PRINCESS with him!
Molly Oh, Jack! What are we going to do!?
Jack Do? Why, go after them of course! All aboard the *Pretty Polly*!
All HURRAH!

9. Song (All)

This should be a stirring "call to arms" number for all those on stage. Finally, Jack is hoisted on to the shoulders of two sailors and strikes a dramatic pose with drawn sword. The others group on either side of Jack for a grand tableau. On the last note of music——

the CURTAIN *falls*

ACT II

Scene 1

The Deck of the "Pretty Polly"

Across the back of the stage are the bulwarks of the ship, high enough for Morac and her Demons to create the impression of having risen from the sea well below deck level. A large sea-chest placed against the bulwarks can serve as a step down. At R, steps lead up to the bridge. At L, are barrels, bales and coils of rope. The backcloth shows blue sky. The side wings represent masts, sails and rigging

The chorus are discovered. The sailors are going about their duties, swabbing the deck, splicing ropes, etc. The others are grouped about the stage

10. Song (Chorus)

After the song, Granfer Fuddlewick appears on the bridge. He wears an outsize naval uniform with dangling sword and huge cocked hat. On his shoulder is a dummy cat concealing a stuffed parrot

Granfer (*saluting*) Ahoy there, shipmates!
All (*saluting back*) Ahoy there, Granfer!

Granfer starts to come down the steps, trips on his sword, falls and rolls on to the deck. Everyone laughs and some of the sailors help him up. Comic business as he readjusts his sword

Sailor (*pointing to the "cat"*) What's that?
Granfer That be the ship's cat!
Sailor What happened to your parrot?
Granfer Inside the cat! See! (*He whips off the "cat" to reveal the parrot. He throws the "cat" off-stage R. Doing a "Long John Silver"*) HA HAR! HA HAR! Mangle me mainstays an' crumple me capstan! 'Tis a fine morning fer bobbin' on the briny an' wobblin' on the waves! Avast there, mateys! 'Ow about a good old fashioned 'ornpipe to scrape the barnacles off yer bottom! (*Coming forward to the Conductor or Pianist*) Lay it on wi' a will, Jim Lad!

11. Hornpipe (Granfer and Sailors)

The Sailors dance a hornpipe. Granfer joins in, gets it all wrong and is roughly ejected by the sailors. He hobbles out down L. The sailors continue the hornpipe with great expertise, clapped on by the others. The barmaids can join in with the dance if so desired. After the dance, the sailors and chorus exit R and L

Jack and Molly enter on the bridge. Jack scans the auditorium through his telescope

Molly Any sign of Jasper Grasper's ship, Jack?
Jack (*snapping the 'scope shut*) Not a speck!

Jack and Molly come down the steps to the deck

That scurvy landlubber had too good a start on us! And what with that confounded fog yesterday and the day before . . . (*He makes a despairing gesture*)
Molly Jack, do you think we'll ever see Princess Valtina again?
Jack Of course we will, my dear! Trust in Captain Jack Dauntless! As long as I've got a ship under me, I'll never give up looking for her!

Granfer enters from down L, *sees Jack and, pulling himself to attention, salutes*

Granfer Ahoy, Cap'n!
Jack (*saluting*) Ahoy, Granfer! At ease!

Granfer slumps "at ease" and almost falls over

Granfer Oi've got some news fer 'ee, Miss Muffet. Ole Dolly Drinkup be comin' up on deck!
Molly Poor Aunty! It'll be the first time she's been out of her cabin since we set sail. She's been very sea-sick!
Granfer Ar! An' oi bet the sea be very sick of 'er! (*He looks off* L) Look out! Thar she blows!

They clear to down R

To suitable music, Dame Drinkup enters from down L. *She trots on, blowing a whistle and high stepping like a games mistress. The children trot on behind her in single file. She takes them for a "run" around the stage. The Dame ends up in the centre and the children form a straight line* L. *She proceeds to do knee-bending exercises and falls on her rump with a thump*

Dame Ooo! (*She sits up, showing "Union Jack" panties*) COR! Talk about striking yer colours! (*To the front row of the audience, pulling down her skirt to cover her panties*) Naughty! You mustn't look when me flag's at half-mast! (*To the others*) Well, help me up somebody!
Granfer (*scuttling across, eagerly*) Oi be comin'! Oi be comin'!
Dame Not you, Captain Birdseye! You keep yer perishin' paws off me!
Granfer (*foiled again*) Spoil-sport!
Dame Go and jiggle yer Jolly Roger if you want something to do.

Molly and Jack help the Dame to her feet

Molly I'm glad you're feeling better, Aunty.
Dame Oh, I am, Molly dear, I am! Never felt better in me life! Yo! Ho! Ho! and a bottle of brown! Ha! Ha! Oh, yes! Now I've got over the collywobbles it's a sailor's life for me! I love the spray around me portholes and the breeze buffetin' me bobstays! Oh, I have the sea in my blood!
Granfer Ar! We can see where it gets in! Hee! Hee!
Dame All I needed was me sea-legs!
Granfer (*looking at her legs*) Be that what you call 'em! Looks like a couple o' *table* legs to oi! Hee! Hee!

His cackle is short-lived because Dame Drinkup grabs him

Dame Listen to me, you pesky Popeye, any more cracks and I'll splice yer mainbrace! (*She lets him drop with a bang*)

Laughing, Jack and Molly exit up the steps and disappear on to the bridge

The children start to sneak off down L

(*Calling to the children*) Oy! You lot! Where do you think you're goin'. We haven't finished our exercises yet!
Children (*groaning*) Oh, do we have to?
Dame Yes you do! You want to grow up to have a fine physic like mine, don't ya'. (*She flexes her arm muscle, then claps her hands*) Come along! Come along! Let's have you in two straight lines! Jump to it!

She blows her whistle and the children reluctantly form two lines on either side of her and Granfer

(*Looking out at the audience and clicking her tongue in disgust to Granfer*) They look a sickly bunch, don't they?
Granfer (*peering at the audience*) Ar! Proper poorly! Too much beer and baccy, oi' reckon!
Dame You're right, Granfer. (*Pointing out a group in the audience*) Especially that lot over there! They look like the morning after the night before!
Granfer Oi' reckon you ought to get 'em to do some physical jerks along wi' us.
Dame What a good idea! (*To the audience*) Would you like that? Would you like to get physical with me? Oh, you cheeky monkey! Just 'cos I've got me new togs on! Do you like them, by the way? (*She parades up and down*) It's the latest thing from (*local shop*). It makes me look twenty years younger! Now, are you all ready! We'll start with something simple. Arms above your heads! Like this! (*She demonstrates*) Come on! Get 'em up! Get 'em up!

The audience, children and Granfer follow her instructions

(*To someone out front*) No! Right up, dear! That's it! NOW, wave 'em from side to side! Like this! (*She demonstrates, then to someone in the audience*) Your *arms*, dear, your *arms*! Imagine you're all trees with the wind! Side to side! Side to side! (*To someone*) Don't knock her out, ya big bully! Lovely! Now rest! Wasn't that fun? Next, put your arms out to the sides. Like this. (*She demonstrates*) Good! (*To someone*) Oy! Stop trying to tickle her, you naughty boy! Now, do this! (*She demonstrates bringing her arms in and out again*) In and out! In and out! In and out! In and ... ooo!

Granfer, in his exuberance, has thumped her in the belly. She doubles up. Granfer cackles

(*Recovering, to Granfer in a high-pitched wheeze*) Stand over there! (*She points to down* L)
Granfer Eh?
Dame (*recovering her voice and bellowing*) STAND OVER THERE!!

Granfer scuttles over and stands at the end of the left line of children

(*To the audience*) Did you all enjoy that? Next, we'll touch our toes!
Granfer Oh, that be easy!

He lifts his foot and touches his toes. The children laugh

Dame What's that? Aerobics?
Granfer No! Rheumatics! (*He clutches his hip in agony*)
Dame Well, it's not done like that anyway, you crazy old clot! You do it like this! (*She bends and touches her toes a couple of times. On the second time she has her back to the audience and shows off her "Union Jack" knickers*)
Granfer (*to the audience*) That proves BRITAIN BE ALL BEHIND!
Dame (*facing front*) THERE! Wasn't I good? I'm ever so flexible!
Granfer (*moving back to* C) Oi bet you can't stay down there fer long.
Dame Oh, yes I can! WATCH THIS!

She bends again with her rear towards Granfer. With a wicked wink at the audience, he slowly draws his sword

SEE! I can stay like this for two hours. I've set myself a target.
Granfer So 'ave oi! BULLSEYE!!

He jabs the tip of his sword into her bottom. Dame Drinkup yells and hops about holding her rear. The children and Granfer howl with laughter

Dame (*to Granfer, rolling up her sleeves for action*) YOU!!! (*She chases Granfer in and out of the children yelling for his blood*)

He just manages to escape off down L

(*Rubbing her painful rear; to the audience*) COR! I think he's punctured me PIRELLI!

The children are now in a group C

1st Boy Have we finished our exercises now, Dame Drinkup?
Dame No, you haven't!
Children (*groaning*) Oo!
Dame You lazy lot of little layabouts! I want to do press-ups next!
Children (*groaning*) Oh, no!
Dame Oh, yes! I'll just get limbered up a bit.

She "limbers" up and the children get into a huddle

1st Girl We've got to do something or she'll have us doing horrible exercises all day!
2nd Boy I wish she was still sea-sick!

The others agree

1st Boy Of course! That's it! I'll soon fix *her*! (*He moves over to the Dame*) Er ... Dame Drinkup?
Dame (*still limbering*) Yes, dear?
1st Boy Are you sure you still don't feel sea-sick?
Dame (*stopping her antics*) Eh? What do you mean?

The children, catching on to the 1st Boy's plan, move over slightly

1st Boy We don't think you look very well. (*To the others with a wink*) Do
we?
Children No!
3rd Boy You look a bit green!
Dame (*alarmed*) Green! Do I?
Children Yes!
Dame (*to the audience*) Do I look green?

The children signal the audience to say "Yes"

    (*Feeling her face*) Oh, dear! Oo! Come to think of it, I ... I do feel a bit
    queasy!
1st Boy It's the roll of the ship that does it. (*With appropriate movements*)
UP AND DOWN! UP AND DOWN!
Children (*joining in*) UP AND DOWN! UP AND DOWN! UP AND
DOWN!

The Dame moves with them, holding her stomach and rolling her eyes

Dame Oo! Stop it! Stop it! Oh! I'm feelin' proper poorly again! Oo!

The children giggle

1st Boy (*to finish her off completely*) We haven't seen you at mealtimes,
Dame Drinkup?
Dame (*gulping*) No, me tummy's been away for a few days! Oh, don't
mention food to me!
4th Boy Sorry to bring it up!
Dame And don't mention *that*, either! Ooo!

12. Song (Children)

*The children sing their song straight at Dame Drinkup, emphasizing all the
food stuffs mentioned. She groans and tries to escape off-stage but they pull her
back*

    It ends with the Dame bursting off-stage down L *with her hand over her
    mouth*

The children roar with laughter

    After the applause, Dame Drinkup staggers back on from down L, *bow-
    legged and cross-eyed*

1st Boy (*innocently*) Shall we go on with the exercises now, Dame Drinkup?
Dame (*weakly*) No ... no more exercises.

*The children shake hands with the 1st Boy and pat him on the back. He bows to
them*

    (*Groaning*) Oo! Stop the bus I want to get off! Ooo!

*Jack and Molly appear on the bridge and come down the steps. At the back a
couple of sailors saunter on, lean on the bulwarks and look out to sea*

Molly Good gracious, Aunty. What's the matter?
Dame (*staggering over to them*) Oh, Molly dear! I've got the jim-jams again!
Captain, can't you find some nice solid land to bump into? I'd love to be

on *dry land again*! Even (*local town*) on a wet weekend! (*She starts crying on Molly's shoulder*) I want to go home! Waaaa!
Sailor (*at the back*) A SAIL! A SAIL!

The cry of "A SAIL!" is repeated loudly off-stage. Jack, Dame, Molly and the children rush up to the bulwarks and look out to sea. Jack uses his telescope

With lots of noise Granfer and the chorus rush on from R *and* L *and go to the bulwarks*

Fishermen (*at back, pointing off up* L) LOOK! A SHIP!
Jack (*looking through his 'scope*) It's JASPER GRASPER'S SHIP!
All HURRAH!
Dame (*grabbing the 'scope*) Let's 'ave a butcher's! Oh, I can see the Princess, poor thing! An' ... an' I can see old Grasper himself! He's waving at us! At least ... I *think* he's wavin'. (*She peers closer*) Oh, how rude! (*She shouts off*) And the same to you, with knobs on!
Jack (*calling*) AHOY THERE! JASPER GRASPER! CAN YOU HEAR ME?
Grasper (*calling back from off, upstage* L) I CAN HEAR YOU! WHAT DO YOU WANT?
Jack (*calling*) I COMMAND YOU TO SURRENDER PRINCESS VALTINA AT ONCE!
Grasper (*off*) HA! HA! THREATEN AWAY, FOOLS! I WILL NEVER GIVE HER UP! NEVER!
Jack I'll send a warning shot across his bows!
Granfer Hee! Hee! That sounds painful!
Jack (*moving away from the bulwarks*) GUNNERS!

Some sailors step forward and spring to attention

Sailors AY, AY, SIR!
Jack Make ready! On the word of command—one warning shot across their bows! JUMP TO IT!
Sailors AY, AY, SIR!

They salute and run out up R

Dame and Granfer move to Jack

Dame Is there goin' to be a big bang, Captain?
Jack (*returning to the bulwarks*) YES!

Dame and Granfer move down L *and cower there, with their eyes shut tight and their fingers in their ears*

(*Calling*) THIS IS YOUR LAST CHANCE, GRASPER! SURRENDER THE PRINCESS OR SUFFER THE CONSEQUENCES!
Grasper (*off*) HA! HA! YOU DON'T SCARE ME! DO YOUR WORST!
Jack (*stepping back and calling to off up* R) Number one gun! FIRE!!

Off-stage, the cannon fires with a tremendous roar and Granfer and Dame Drinkup fall over

All HURRAH!
Jack Ha! Ha! That's shaken them up a bit!

Dame (*sitting up and adjusting her chest*) You can say that again! (*She joins the others at the bulwarks*)

Jack (*looking through his scope*) They've lowered a boat! They're bringing the Princess!

All HURRAH!

Jack (*moving away from the bulwarks*) MEN! Stand by to receive boarders!

Three sailors shout "AY, AY, SIR!" and run out up L

Everyone leaves the bulwarks

(*To all*) Avast there, shipmates! Prepare to welcome Princess Valtina on board! Here she comes!

All cheer as the Spider rushes on from up L *and goes straight to Molly, Jack and Dame Drinkup. They greet her warmly*

Spider (*overjoyed*) My dear friends! My dear, dear friends I thought I would never see you again!

The three sailors enter from up L, *escorting Flip and Flop and a very morose Jasper Grasper. Flip and Flop now wear comic nautical attire*

Jack (*moving downstage, to the sailors, sternly*) BRING THEM HERE!

The sailors push Flip and Flop and they fall to their knees before Jack. Grasper remains standing, his arms folded in defiance

Jack (*to Flip and Flop*) NOW! What have you to say for yourselves?

Flip (*frightened*) It . . . it wasn't us!

Flop No, *we* didn't want to kidnap her! It was *him*!

He points to Grasper, who snarls back

Flip Yes, he made us do it! (*To the audience*) Didn't he?

Audience YES!

Grasper (*to the audience, moving forwards*) Oh, no, I didn't!

Audience Oh, yes, you did!

Grasper Oh, no, I didn't!!

This continues until Jack calls a halt

Jack BELAY!

Grasper (*sneering at Jack*) Ha! You may have won this round, but don't think you've got the better of Jasper Grasper! Oh, no! I mean to have that talking spider and no jumped-up cabin boy will stop me!

Jack (*to a sailor*) Take him below and clap him in irons! (*To Grasper*) As soon as we return to England, you shall stand trial for KIDNAPPING! Take him away!

The sailor drags Grasper out down L. *He shakes his fist at those on-stage and the audience as he goes*

(*To the chorus, pointing to Flip and Flop*) What shall we do with these two swabs?

Sailor Feed 'em to the sharks!

All YES!

Flip and Flop cringe with fear

Spider No, you mustn't! (*To Jack*) They are telling the truth. *They* didn't want to kidnap me. They were just carrying out that awful man's instructions. Please let them go free, Captain Dauntless.

Jack (*reluctantly*) Well, if you say so, your highness. (*To Flip and Flop, sternly*) You've been let off—and think yourself lucky!

Flip and Flop get to their feet, expressing relief and thanks

Sailor (*at the bulwarks, pointing out to sea*) LAND HO! LAND HO!

Everyone rushes up to the bulwarks and peers out to sea

Jack (*looking through his 'scope*) It's land all right, I wonder——

Suddenly the Spider squeals with delight and dances downstage excitedly. All turn and look at her in amazement

(*Concerned*) Your highness!

Dame She's gone bonkers!

Spider It's VALADOR! IT'S VALADOR! IT'S MY HOME! MY HOME!

Jack VALADOR! Are you sure, Princess?

Spider Oh, YES, YES! I'd know it anywhere! VALADOR! MY HOME! HURRAH!!

She grabs Dame Drinkup in her wild excitement, and spins her round. Everyone is as overjoyed as the Spider

Jack (*calling them to order*) AVAST THERE! BELAY! SHIP'S COMPANY! MAKE READY! OUR NEXT STOP—THE KINGDOM OF VALADOR!

All HURRAH!

Spider (*hugging Molly and the Dame*) At last! I'm going home!

Jack Yes, and there's no place like it!

13. Song (Jack, Molly, Spider and chorus)

After the number, there is a binding flash of lightning and a tremendous clap of thunder. The Lighting grows dark and eerie

Morac (*laughing demoniacally on the off-stage microphone*) HA! HA! HA! HA!

Spider (*in terror*) That laugh! It's Morac! Morac, the witch!

Sailor (*pointing to the back*) LOOK!

They all spin around, and shrink to the sides in mute terror

Weird flickering lights seem to be coming from the sea. A ghostly mist covers the deck. Strange noises fill the air. Morac's laugh is heard, and her nightmarish Demons appear over the bulwarks and jump to the deck

14. Demon Dance (Demons)

In the mist the Demons perform a wild dance. On the last note of music they fall to their knees, facing upstage. They raise their arms, heralding the approach of their queen

There is another flash of lightning and a roll of thunder. Slowly, Morac appears above the bulwarks. She rises out of the mist, a terrifying figure with arms outstretched

All the Demons bow in homage

Morac (*laughing demonically*) HA! HA! HA! HA!
Spider (*clinging to Molly in terror*) IT'S HER! IT'S MORAC! OH, SAVE ME! SAVE ME!

Still laughing, Morac descends to the deck and the strange noises fade into the background

Morac   Beware, wretched mortals, ere you look on me.
I am MORAC, the Queen of Sorcery!
I see you have the Princess here, I turned her into a spider!
She foolishly ran away from me and hid where I couldn't find her!
But now she's in my grasp again, she won't escape this time!
I'll conjure up a mighty storm, the best in Pantomime!
This ship of yours will be a wreck, no one on board I'll save!
No christmas pud for you next year, just a lovely watery grave!
HA! HA! HA! HA!

All are panic-stricken. Jack steps forward with drawn sword

Jack   Begone foul witch and leave my ship!
We'll hear no more of your old lip!
Morac   You can't stop ME, you headstrong brat!
(*Sneering*) Your sword is useless—TAKE THAT!

She points her wand at Jack. A strange whirring noise seems to come from the wand. Special lighting (strobe if possible) flashes across the stage. Jack appears to be struggling with some mighty invisible force, and he is thrown backwards. With a triumphant laugh, Morac lowers her wand. The whirring noises and flashing lights fade as she does so

HA! HA! HA!
You see! From your attempts I am immune!
Now to raise a great typhoon!

Laughing, she goes to the back and stands on the sea-chest. With out-stretched arms, she casts her awful spell. The Demons join her at the back, waving their arms about in "voodoo" fashion

(*Chanting*)
O, serpents and devils of the sea,
I command you arise, and work for me!

Monstrous roars and bellowings are heard on the off-stage microphone

Make waves as big as mountains rise!
This ship I want to pulverize!
Drag it down to the deepest sea bed.
And make sure these fools are well and truly DEAD!!
HA! HA! HA! HA!

There is a blinding flash and Morac and her Demons disappear over the bulwarks and vanish into the mist

Storm music. The ship is now in the grips of a terrible tempest. Thunder and lightning, howling winds, crashing waves—the works! Bits of mast, rigging and canvas fall to the deck. Everyone is being thrown about, yelling and screaming. All is uproar. Jack desperately tries to keep order

Granfer runs off upstage L

Jack (*shouting above the din*) KEEP CALM! MAN THE LIFEBOATS! DON'T PANIC! MAN THE LIFEBOATS!

Dame (*clinging to Molly and Spider*) Oo! Call the waterboard! Call a plumber! Help! S.O.S.! Women and landladies first! Ooo!

Granfer staggers in from down L, *with the broken ship's wheel hanging around his neck*

Quick Black-out. The storm noises continue into the next scene

SCENE 2

The Weird Woods of Valador

Tabs, or a frontcloth showing an eerie, dense wood, full of twisted trees and weird looking plants. Strange, eerie lighting. The storm noises gradually fade away

The Demons leap on from down R *and* L

There is a flash of lightning, a roll of thunder and Morac enters from L

Morac HA! HA! HA! HA! (*To the audience*)
　　　　　My magic raised a tempest wild, the ship now lies on the bottom!
　　　　　The Princess and her stupid friends are drowned and the sharks
　　　　　　　have got 'em!
　　　　　HA! HA! HA! HA!

There is a flash on R, *and the Good Fairy appears*

The Demons recoil and shrink away from her

Fairy　　Oh, no Wicked Witch, they did not drown,
　　　　　They are safe on Valador,
　　　　　I saved them ere the ship went down,
　　　　　And placed them on the shore. (*She points off* R)
Morac (*looking off*)
　　　　　Ah! 'tis true! But who are you, to meddle with my magic?
Fairy　　I thought it time I showed myself, as things were getting tragic!
　　　　　(*To the audience*) Allow me to present myself. I am the Good Kind
　　　　　　Fairy.
　　　　　It is my job to come along, when things are looking scary.
Morac (*moving to the Fairy and sneering*)
　　　　　Ha! You may have saved them from the sea,
　　　　　But do not think I'm through!
　　　　　I've still got lots of magic that will scare the pants off you!
　　　　　(*To the audience*)
　　　　　I'll find them all, just wait and see!

They won't get far away from me!
(*To the Fairy*)
Against my power you have no hope!
You're just a puny little dope!
HA! HA! HA!

Laughing, she sweeps out down L, *followed by cackling Demons*

Fairy (*to the audience*)
Alas, the things she says are true.
I'll be completely frank with you!

She turns and shows the audience an "L" plate on her back

You see! I haven't even passed my test.
I'm still a learner fairy-est!
If I were now a full blown sprite,
I'd give that Morac such a fright!
But I will help as best I can,
To foil the Witch's evil plan;
As everything has turned out wrong,
I'll cheer you up with this little song!

15. Song and Dance (Fairy)

The Fairy can end the song with a little dance, after which she exits down R

The children enter from down L, *and look nervously about them, a bedraggled, frightened group*

1st Girl (*to 1st Boy*) W-where are we?
1st Boy (*with false bravado*) Well, it's not (*local park or shopping precinct*) that's for sure!
2nd Boy What happened?
1st Boy (*exasperated*) For the hundredth time, I tell you I *don't* know! There was a storm! The ship sank and we found ourselves on the beach.
2nd Girl (*to 1st Boy*) But what's happened to Captain Dauntless, and the others?
1st Boy (*looking heavenwards*) Give me strength!
4th Girl (*snivelling*) I—I don't like this place. I'm s-scared! I want to go home!

She starts wailing. Some of the other girls comfort her. The boys groan

4th Boy Trust a stupid girl to start bawling!
1st Boy (*to crying girl*) Oh, put a sock in it!

The Girl wails even louder

1st Girl (*hotly, to 1st Boy*) Don't talk to her like that!

The boys and girls start a loud, heated argument. They do not see . . .

The Demons as they creep on from R *and* L. *They are now armed with evil-looking spears. Two of them carry a long rope. They advance slowly on the unsuspecting children, and surround them*

One of the girls spots the Demons and gives a piercing scream

1st Boy RUN FOR IT!!

Too late! Cackling, the Demons close in, jabbing at the children with their spears and herd them into a tight group. The two Demons with the rope run around the children and tie them up

Morac sweeps on from down R, *laughing her terrible laugh*

Morac Ha! Ha! Ha!
          So! The little brats have been caught first,
          Bind them tight until they burst!
1st Boy We've just one thing to say to you!
All Children
          ON YER BIKE! YOU SILLY OLD MOO!
Morac (*enraged*)
          Ah! For that remark you'll cringe and cower!
          DRAG THEM OFF TO MY DARK TOWER!

The two Demons haul the roped children off down L. *Morac and the others follow. She pokes her tongue out at the audience and exits down* L

The Lights fade to Black-out

SCENE 3

The Seashore of Valador

The backcloth shows sea, sky and beach framed by trees and jungle. Side wings represent dense jungle, exotic plants, creepers, etc. Mid-stage L, *there is a tall rock with roughly carved steps leading to a wide stone ledge. Near the base of the steps there is a low, flat rock big enough for three persons to sit side by side*

To suitable music, the Lights come up on an empty stage. Suddenly a large gorilla makes its entrance, giving the audience a fright. If possible, it can swing in from the wings on a camouflaged rope or leap from the stone ledge, landing onstage with a loud bang. It thumps its chest then catches sight of the audience. It gives a questioning grunt then ambles up and down, trying to make verbal contact with them. It is about to climb down into the audience when voices off-stage attract its attention

Flip (*off* L, *calling*) YOO HOO!
Flop (*off* R, *calling*) TYPHOO!

The Gorilla climbs back onstage and hides behind the tall rock

Flip (*off* L, *calling in sing-song voice*) HELLOO! WHERE ARE YOOO?
Flop (*off* R, *replying in sing-song voice*) I'M OVER HERE! WHERE ARE YOO HOO!

Flip enters backwards from down L. *Simultaneously, Flop enters backwards down* R. *They both move slowly towards* C, *looking furtively from side to side. Eventually, their bottoms touch and they both freeze, terror-stricken. They turn slowly, see each other and yell in fright*

W-w-where are we?
Flip How should I know! The last thing I remember was the ship sinking.

Flop Same here! Hey! (*He clings to Flip*) Perhaps, we're (*he gulps*) deaded!

Flip Well, that should'nt worry *you*! You've been deaded for years! (*He moves up behind Flop, looking off* R)

Flop (*knees knocking with fear*) I-I don't l-like it here! It's sp-spooky! I'm sc-scared!

Flip (*right behind Flop and bellowing to off* R) HELLO!

Flop (*leaping with fright*) AHHH! DON'T DO DAT!

Flip This must be Valador, Princess Valtina's home. That's where we were heading when the Old Witch did a (*TV weatherman/woman*) and gave us wet and windy in all areas! You remember the Witch, don't you?

Flop Hilda Ogden's granny, you mean? I should say I do! (*Shaking again*) Oo! I hope she isn't hidin' around here!

Flip I wonder what happened to the others? Do you think they were all drowned in the storm? Perhaps we're the only ones to survive! Just you and me, macarooned on a desert island!

Flop And not even a "Bounty" bar between us!

Flip (*putting his arm around Flop*) If that *is* the case, old mate, we've got to be brave!

Flop (*shaking*) Oh, I don't want to stop here! We might get eaten by cannon balls! What are we goin' to do?!

Flip Let's sit down and try to think of a way out of here.

They move to the low flat rock and sit at each end, back to back in the attitude of Rodin's "Thinker". The Gorilla creeps from behind the tall rock and moves down behind them. If the audience call out Flip and Flop take no notice. The Gorilla stands looking from one to the other, then taps Flip on the shoulder

(*Without moving*) What?

Flop (*without moving*) What what?

Flip What do you want?

Flop I don't want anything!

They go back to deep thinking. The Gorilla taps Flop on the shoulder

Yes?

Flip Yes, what?

Flop Yes please! What do you want?

Flip I don't want anything! Keep thinking!

The Gorilla scratches its head, then sits between Flip and Flop. It looks from one to the other and then proceeds to examine the back of Flip's head

(*Slapping the Gorilla's paw away without turning*) Stop that!

Flop Stop what?

Flip That!

The Gorilla now turns its attention to the back of Flop's head. Flop starts giggling

Flop (*squirming*) Stop it! You know I'm ticklish!

The Gorilla tickles him in the ribs. Flop is helpless with laughter

Flip Behave yourself! Keep thinking!

The Gorilla stops tickling Flop. A slight pause. Bored, the Gorilla gives a deep

38

sigh. Simultaneously, Flip and Flop turn to face front, crossing their legs as they do so. The Gorilla copies them. All three sit with crossed legs. Slight pause. All three give one loud sigh, then quickly re-cross their legs

Have you thought of anything?

The Gorilla shakes its head

Flop Nope. Have you?

The Gorilla shakes its head again

Flip No. It's hopeless, isn't it?

The Gorilla nods its head and gives a grunt

Flip You can say that again!

Flop looks puzzled for a second. All three sigh heavily again. The Gorilla puts its arms around them

Ah, you're a great comfort to me, old mate.
Flop And *you're* a great comfort to *me*, old mate.

Together they pat the Gorilla's paw on their shoulders. The Gorilla kisses Flip on the cheek

Flip (*pulling away in disgust and wiping his cheek*) Oy! There's no need for that!
Flop (*puzzled*) What?
Flip That what you did!
Flop What did I did?
Flip You ... you kissed me!
Flop I ... (*He starts laughing*) I kissed *you!* Ha! Ha! I'd sooner kiss (*politician*).

He rocks with laughter. The Gorilla copies him in mime. Flip has turned away in disgust. Flop clings to the Gorilla in helpless laughter. All of a sudden he becomes aware of the Gorilla. Comic business with him gaping at the Gorilla and then at the audience in mute terror. He tries to pull away but the ape holds him tightly. He manages to utter a strangled gurgle

Flip It's no good saying sorry. I don't want to know!

Flop gurgles again

No! I'm finished with you! You've made a fool of me for the last time! We'll go our separate ways from now on! *I'm leaving!*

He gets up and goes to move off, but the Gorilla reaches out and grabs him firmly by the ankle

(*Without looking, his nose in the air*) Don't try to stop me! I said I'm leaving and I mean it! Let go of me! Stop monkeying about!

He bends down to free his ankle. He looks at the hairy paw, then at the hairy arm, then at the hairy Gorilla! In mute terror he gapes from the Gorilla to the audience. He and Flop both make strangled, gurgling noises. Eventually they find their voices, and scream

Flip } (*together*)   Ahhhhh!!
Flop

Startled, the Gorilla lets them go and they fall over

Leaping to their feet they run out R, *yelling with terror*

The Gorilla watches them go, scratching its head in puzzlement. It gets up and ambles off down L, *shaking its head in disbelief*

Dame (*off up* R, *calling*) YOO HOO! COOEE! ANYONE AT HOME!

She staggers on from up R, *looking very bedraggled and very lost*

DING DONG, AVON CALLING! SHOP! (*She wanders down, sees the audience and rushes forward*) Oh, thank goodness—civilization at last! (*She peers at the audience*) Oh, no, it's not! It's just you lot again! Oh, what a time I've 'ad! The poor old ship went down and me along with it! I woke up on that beach covered in seaweed, shells and sprats! (*She wriggles about*) In fact . . . I . . . I think there's one still around somewhere! (*She fishes down the neck of her costume and wriggles about*) Yes . . . yes! It's down there, playin' at sardines! (*She extracts a rubber fish*) There! Oooooops! (*The fish slips from her fingers and goes out into the audience*) There you are, dear, get a few chips and you're in business! Ha! Ha! Ha! (*Sudden gloom*) Oh, but I don't know why I'm laughing! I'm that worried! What's happened to all the others! Perhaps, I'm the only one left! A caraway on a desert island! (*She moves down* L, *very melodramatic*) Oh, woe is me! Woe is me!

Jasper Grasper enters backwards from down R. *He wears only his top hat, old-fashioned combinations and a short grass skirt. He turns to face front, not seeing Dame Drinkup*

Oh, look! It's Aunty Beattie from old Tahiti!
Grasper (*crossing to her eagerly*) Ah! A survivor!
Dame (*dodging past him*) Yes, and I'm goin' to stay that way!
Grasper (*pursuing her*) Dame Drinkup!
Dame (*standing her ground*) Keep away from me!
Grasper (*taking a step nearer*) Come here!
Dame I warn you! I've got a lawn-mower in me bag!
Grasper (*advancing on her*) Come here!
Dame (*backing away*) Don't come near me, you . . . you Shredded Wheat, you! Ooo!

He chases her around. She falls over and he drags her to her feet

Oh, unhand me, sir! You don't want *me*! I've gone over the "sell by" date!
Grasper Tell me! Where is the talking spider! Is it alive? Where is it? (*He shakes her roughly*) Tell me! Where is it? SPEAK! SPEAK! WHERE IS IT?
Dame (*being shook*) St-stop it! St-stop sh-shaking me about! I'll g-g-go all f-f-fizzy! Oo!
Grasper (*stopping shaking her*) Where is that talking spider?
Dame I don't know! When I woke up on the beach I was all on me tod!
Grasper (*releasing her*) So! If we managed to escape the storm, there is a

good chance that the Spider did also! If it is here, I will find it! I'll search every crook and nanny! Then it will be mine! ALL MINE! (*He dances on the spot, laughing with devilish glee*) Ha! Ha! Ha! Ha!

Dame (*reacting*) Oy! Oy! Stop that! I'm gettin'covered in greenfly!

Grasper controls himself

Gracias!

Grasper Don't be personal! (*He goes down* L)

Dame Hey, little weed! Where are you goin'?

Grasper (*rubbing his hands melodramatically*) I'm going to find my TALK-ING SPIDER! (*He turns to go*)

Dame (*rushing to him in a panic*) WAIT! YOU CAN'T LEAVE ME HERE ALONE! Me, a poor, defenceless girl, a prey to savages and wild beasts! (*Grabbing him*) We might be the only ones left alive! We're all we've got! I know you're a nasty man, but I think I could get to like you—(*looking at his grass skirt*)—you snake in the grass, you!

Grasper (*pulling away*) ARR!

Dame (*pulling him back*) And I KNOW you could get to like ME! *I've got so much to offer!*

16. Comedy Song (Dame and Jasper)

At the end of the song Grasper pushes her over and runs out down L

(*Getting up and rubbing her rear*) MEN! TYPICAL! They always let you down! (*She limps to the low rock and sits*) Oh, I'm so tired! (*She gives a big yawn*) I'm proper pooped! I think I'll have forty winks. (*She lies out on the rock*) Give us a shout if you see anything. NIGHT-NIGHT! (*She puts her thumb in her mouth and goes to sleep, snoring loudly*)

The Gorilla enters from R. *It sees Dame Drinkup and creeps slowly towards her*

The audience will be shouting "Wake up", "Gorilla", etc. The Dame wakes with a start and sits up

(*To the audience*) W-what is it? What's up?

She gets up and comes forward. The Gorilla is behind her

(*To the audience*) What is it?

Audience A GORILLA!

Dame A GORILLA! W-WHERE?

Audience BEHIND YOU!

Comic business with her turning round slowly and the Gorilla keeping behind her. "Oh, no there isn't" "Oh, yes there is" routine

Dame (*facing the audience*) Well, I can't see one! (*She talks absently to the Gorilla who is now standing beside her*) This dopey lot says there's a GORILL——Ahhhhhhhhhhhh!

She runs to and fro in sheer panic. The Gorilla chases her

(*Yelling at the top of her voice*) HELP! IT'S AFTER ME! HELP! TARZAN, WHERE ARE YOU! HELP! SAVE ME!

She trips and falls near the low rock. The Gorilla grabs her by the foot. She clings to the rock, yelling blue murder

Jack (*off* L, *calling*) DAME DRINKUP? IS THAT YOU?
Molly (*off* L, *calling*) AUNT DOLLY? WHERE ARE YOU?

Hearing the voices, the Gorilla drops Dame Drinkup's foot and scampers out down L

The Dame continues to cling to the rock, holding her leg out and yelling for all she is worth

Jack, Molly and Granfer appear on the stone ledge and run down the steps. At the same time the chorus run in from R. *Everyone pulls up short and is puzzled by the strange spectacle of Dame Drinkup*

Dame (*struggling with thin air*) AH! HE'S GOT ME! HE'S GOT ME! HELP!

Molly goes and kneels beside Dame Drinkup. She puts a soothing hand on her shoulder

Molly Aunty ... Aunty?

The Dame stops struggling and looks up at Molly

Dame Molly? Is it you?
Molly Yes, wha's the matter?
Dame I ... (*She looks towards her foot, then gives a big sigh of relief*) Phew! It's gone! (*She sits up*)
Jack What was it?
Dame A great hairy GORILLA! It must have been KING KONG! I thought it was goin' to pick me up and carry me off!

Molly helps her up

Granfer (*to a villager*) T'would take more than King Kong to pick 'er up! He! He! He!
Dame Oh, Molly dear, thank goodness you're safe! I thought you'd all been drowned. (*Looking around*) But ... but where's Princess Valtina?
Molly We don't know.
Jack (*sadly*) I'm afraid it looks as though Princess Valtina was either drowned or captured by the Witch!
Sailor (*pointing off* R) LOOK!

Flip and Flop enter from R, *with the Spider*

All HURRAH!

The Spider runs to Molly and the others who greet her warmly, ad lib

Flip We found her wandering in the jungle.
Dame (*to the Spider*) You'd better watch out, Princess, that nasty old Jasper Grasper's still about and he's looking for you!
Jack That scurvy landlubber! Fear not, Princess! He'll not touch you as long as I'm here! (*Slaps his thigh*)
Dame I'll second that! (*She bares her thigh and slaps it*)

Granfer An' oi'll *third* it!

He goes to slap Dame Drinkup's thigh but she pushes him away

Molly (*to Jack*) But what about Morac! By now she'll know we escaped the storm and she'll be coming after us!

Jack (*his hand on his sword*) Let her come!

Spider You are very brave Captain Dauntless, but you are no match against her evil powers. You have all been through so much for my sake, but now it must end. I will go to Morac and give myself up. That way, you will be spared from any further danger.

Jack Princess, we have come too far to desert you now. We'll stand by you to the end!

All Ay!!

Suddenly, there is a flash of lightning and a great clap of thunder. The stage grows dark and eerie

Morac (*laughing on the off-stage microphone*) HA! HA! HA! HA!

> *To suitable music, Morac's Demons leap on from down* L. *They force Jack and the others over to* R, *then gather at the base of the steps*

> *There is another flash of lightning, a roll of thunder and Morac appears on the stone ledge*

Morac   HA! HA! HA! HA!
So, you fools, we meet again! The battle has not ended!
I've come to claim the Princess there and kill her as intended!
If anyone stands in my way or gives me any trouble,
I'll conjure up a thunderbolt and blast you all to rubble!

Slowly, she descends the steps. The Spider pulls away from Molly and Jack

Molly Princess, no . . .

Jack Don't do it, your highness!

Spider (*turning to them, calmly*) I must, I will have no-one hurt on my account.

With great dignity, she walks towards Morac. Two of the Demons grab her and drag her before Morac, who remains on the steps

(*To Morac, proudly*) I, Princess Valtina of Valador surrender to you. You are free to do with *me* as you wish, but let these good people go free and unharmed.

Morac   HA! HA! HA! (*With scorn*)
Who are you to order me!
I, the queen of sorcery!
I'll do with them as I see fit!
I'll burn them all in a fiery pit!

All react in terror

But no! I know what would be nice!
I'll turn them all to blocks of ice!
HA! HA! HA!

Morac points her wand at the group. The whirring noise is heard and lights flash across the stage. Jack, Molly and the others are frozen like statues, Dame Drinkup and Granfer in comic attitudes. Morac lowers her wand and the noises and special lights fade

Spider (*trying to pull away from the Demons*) My friends! My friends!
Morac (*descending to stage level*)
        HA! HA! HA!
        You must admit I'm very clever.
        They'll stay like that for ever and ever!

She seizes the Spider

        And now, my beauty, off we go, to my tower up on high.
        For there I hold the King and Queen and with them you shall DIE!
        HA! HA! HA! HA!

Laughing, she drags the Spider up the steps and they disappear along the stone ledge. The Demons follow, cackling with devilish delight

As soon as the last Demon is out of sight the Lights return to normal

There is a flash down L and the Fairy appears

Fairy   Oh, dear, oh, dear, things do look black!
        The Witch now has the Princess!
        I wish that I could get her back,
        But I'm so flippin' useless!

She moves across to the frozen Group

        I can at least help these poor folk,
        She's made them stiff and formal.

She waves her wand over the group

        Come, wakey, wakey, rise and shine,
        Return at once to normal!

She moves away as Jack and the others come back to life. Dame Drinkup and Granfer almost topple over

Molly (*looking towards the steps*) Where's the Princess?
Villager She's gone?
Fisherman (*pointing to the Fairy*) Hey! Look!

They all look and the Fairy tries to adopt a classic fairy pose

Granfer It's Russell Grant!
Fairy (*moving a little nearer to them*)
        Good people, do not be alarmed.
        I've come to give assistance.
        I am a fairy, good and charmed,
        So offer no resistance.
Dame (*dazed*) Fairies! Talkin' spiders! Witches! Gorillas! Crikey, I must be drunk!!
Granfer Oi wish *oi* were!

Molly (*moving to the Fairy*) Good Fairy, can you tell us what has happened to Princess Valtina?

Dame Yes, and in plain English, if you don't mind. None of that—"There was a young lady from Leeds"—stuff! You sound like a pint-size Pam Ayres!

Fairy Oh, thank goodness for that! What a relief! I only do it because people expect it. It's not easy ...

Jack (*earnestly*) Please—tell us about the Princess.

Fairy Well, it's bad news I'm afraid. Morac has taken her to her secret domain. A terrible, evil place from which there is no return.

Dame (*in horror*) Not the (*local disco or night spot*)?

Fairy Much worse than that! She's taken her to the Dark Tower! The King and Queen have been prisoners there for months. Now she has the Princess, Morac plans to kill the entire Royal Household today!

Everyone reacts

Dame Then why haven't *you* done something about it. I thought good fairies were supposed to stop nasty things from happenin'!

Fairy Well, I'm still only a learner. (*She shows her "L" plate*)

Dame (*to the audience*) Just our luck! A faulty fairy!

Molly (*to the fairy*) But, can't you help us at all?

Fairy I can show you the way to the Dark Tower.

Dame Thanks a bundle!

Jack (*to the Fairy*) Then please do! We haven't a second to lose if we're going to save the Royal Family.

Fairy All right. I'll show you.

She moves down L. *Everyone follows and gathers behind her*

(*Pointing off down* L) You see that path? Follow it until you come to the foot of a tall mountain. (*Darkly*) At the summit of this mountain stands Morac's Dark Tower.

> To make this trip you're very plucky,
> We'll meet again—*if* you are lucky!

There is a flash down L *and the Fairy disappears*

Jack (*striding to* C *and taking command*) Come, shipmates! What are we waiting for! (*He draws his sword*) Forward to the Witch's Tower! Today we save the Royal House of Valador!

Stirring music. Led by Jack, everyone marches around the stage, and out down L

Everyone except Dame Drinkup and Flip and Flop! They continue to march around oblivious that the others have gone. Led by Dame Drinkup they march out down R

The Gorilla appears from behind the tall rock and marches out after them

The Lights fade to Black-out

Scene 4

The Weird Woods again

Tabs, or the frontcloth used in Act II, Scene 2

Jasper Grasper enters from down L

Grasper (*to the audience*) BAH! Curse upon curse! I have searched every part of this wretched place and found no sign of that talking spider! But, I'll never give up! Not *I!* Jasper Grasper will not be beaten! I'll find that spider! Oh, yes I will! (*He hears something off* R) What's that! (*He goes to* R *and peers off. He rubs his hands in devilish glee*) Ha! Ha! Someone is coming along the path with my talking spider! I'll hide and wait me chance!

He exits, melodramatically, down L

Morac enters from down R, *dragging the exhausted Spider. Two or three Demons bring up the rear*

Morac   It's not much further, my little dear,
                  Your place of death is very near!
                  Soon your royal blood shall flow.
                  So, let's not linger—on we go!

She pulls the Spider towards L

Grasper leaps out from down L

Grasper   Ha! Ha! At last! My talking spider!
(*To the audience*)   I told you all that I would find her!
(*To Morac*)   I want that spider to put in my show!
                       So, hand her over, you silly old crow!

He grabs one of the Spider's arms. To suitable music, a tug of war follows for possession of the Spider. At last, Grasper succeeds in pulling her away from Morac

                  Ha! Ha! I win! She's mine at last!
Morac   Hold on there, brother. Not so fast!
(*Chanting*)   O scales of dragon, wing of bat,
                  Make him vanish—just like *that!*

She points her wand at Grasper. The whirring noise is heard and lights flash across the stage

There is a Black-out, during which Grasper exits

The Lights return to normal. Laughing triumphantly, Morac seizes the Spider

                  The meddler has gone, and not before time!
                  `There is only one villain in this pantomime!
                  No-one can stop me, for I have the power!
                  Now, on we go to yonder Dark Tower!

Laughing, she sweeps out down L, *dragging the Spider. The Demons follow, snarling and shaking their spears at the audience*

A slight pause, then Flip enters down R, *followed by Dame Drinkup and Flop. All are weary and lost*

Flip Oh, no! We're just going round in circles! We've been *here* before!

Flop How can you tell?

Flip (*pointing out at the audience*) I recognize that funny looking tree stump over there.

Dame (*coming forward and peering at the audience*) Yes! And I've seen those little mushroom things before! (*Melodramatically*) Oh, we're lost! *Lost! LOST!* (*Turning to Flip*) It's all *your* fault! Why didn't you follow Captain Jack and the others, *you wally*!!

Flip Don't you call me names, you ... you person, you!

Dame By now they'll be at the Dark Tower doing battle with Dirty Girtie and we're stuck 'ere playin' *hide and seek*!

Flip If only I could find my bearings!

Dame Oh, you haven't lost them as well! You're hopeless!

Flip (*moving to* L) Let's try this way.

Flip goes out down L

Flop is about to follow; Dame Drinkup stops him

Dame Not you, Medallion Man, you can stay here and keep *me* company. (*Looking about nervously*) Who knows what horrors may be lurkin' in the murkin'. (*She pulls Flop to right of her*)

He creeps away and exits down L

The Gorilla enters from R *and takes Flop's place beside the Dame*

She directs her speech out front, thinking she is talking to Flop. If the audience call out, Dame Drinkup takes no notice in this case

This reminds me of when I was a teensy-weensy toddler. I went to visit my granny who lived in the middle of great big wood. Well, I got lost. I was so scared! I thought some nasty big animal would come along and eat me all up! You can imagine how I felt, can't you?

The Gorilla gives a grunt

Yes. Well, I just sat down and cried my little eyes out!

The Gorilla makes noises

Yes, just like that! Then it started to get dark! Oo! Just the memory of it scares me stiff! You'd better hold my hand, before I can tell you the rest.

She holds out her right hand and the Gorilla takes it

(*Thrilled*) Oo! Aren't you a hairy little man! (*She looks at the Gorilla, does a double-take and screams*) Ahhhhhhhh! IT'S KING KONG AGAIN!!

She struggles to get free, but the Gorilla holds her firmly. He starts to tickle her under the chin. She stops struggling and looks from the Gorilla to the audience

(*To the audience*) I think he fancies me!

The Gorilla releases her and thumps its chest

All right! All right! There's no need to go bananas!

The Gorilla grabs her, and bending her over in a "Valentino" type embrace, kisses her on the cheek

(*To the audience*) Typical! I've been after a feller for years and I end up with a fugitive from P.G. Tips!

The Gorilla pull her up right and thumps its chest again. Dame Drinkup does the same and gives the "Tarzan" call. Jungle-type music starts and the Gorilla goes into a comic dance

17. Gorilla Dance (Gorilla and Dame)

After a few steps on its own, the Gorilla grabs Dame Drinkup and they dance together, ending with a comic tableau

Flip and Flop enter from down L. They see the Gorilla, yell and go to run out again

(*Going to them*) Hey! Come back! Don't be afraid of Ruby Nearenough! He's a friend! (*She drags them towards the Gorilla*) Boys, meet Tarzan's Dad!

Flip and Flop nervously hold their hands out to the Gorilla. It growls at them and they back away

(*To the Gorilla*) Now, don't be jealous! They mean nothing to me! (*To Flip and Flop*) He's *so* POSSESSIVE! Did you find a way out of the wood?
Flop No, it's too dense.
Dame Yes, like you!
Flip (*pointing to the Gorilla*) Perhaps he knows a way.
Flop He might even know the way to the Witch's Tower.
Dame I'll ask him. (*To the Gorilla*) Will you take us to Morac's Dark Tower?

The Gorilla nods

Lead on, Mr Kong!

The Gorilla takes her by the hand and leads her towards R

(*To the audience, as she goes*) David Attenborough—eat your heart out!

She is led off down R by the Gorilla. Flip takes Flop by the hand and leads him off as ...

The Lights fade to Black-out

SCENE 5

Inside Morac's Dark Tower

A dark, sinister place full of evil atmosphere. The backcloth shows slimy grey stone work, cobwebs, a skeleton hanging in chains, and implements of torture

The side wings represent damp, dark walls. A stone bench is set near the R wings. To suitably sinister music, the Lights come up and the eerie scene is revealed

The Demons enter from L, *dragging King Valentine, Queen Valtora and the children. The Royal Pair wear heavy manacles. The King stumbles and falls to his knees. One of the Demons lashes at him with a whip. Two boys push the Demon back as the Queen and some of the children help the King to his feet. They assist him to the stone bench where he and the Queen sit*

Gibbering with devilish glee, the Demons exit L

In despair, the King drops his head into his hands

1st Boy (*to the King*) Please don't give up hope, your majesty.

1st Girl Everything is going to be all right, you'll see.

King (*rising*) Thank you, my young friends. It is very good of you to try and relieve our melancholy, but Queen Valtora and I make very poor companions.

Queen (*rising*) Imprisonment in this foul place has dulled our spirits greatly. For a year we have endured Morac's cruel treatment in the hope that our dear child escaped to safety after being transformed into a spider. That one hope has given us strength.

King But now, after what you have told us, life does not seem worth living any more. (*He puts his arm around the Queen*) My dear, we must be brave and face the awful truth—our little girl is lost to us—forever!

Queen (*weeping*) Oh, my poor, poor Valtina!

The King comforts her. The children exchange concerned glances then do their best to be optimistic

2nd Boy Your majesties, you can't be certain she was drowned in the storm.

2nd Girl She's probably safe in hiding somewhere.

King I wish I could share your optimism, my young friends. But I fear the worse! The Witch's powers are great and terrible. Even if Valtina *did* manage to escape the storm, Morac will by now have sought her out and—and destroyed her!

Morac (*laughing on an off-stage microphone*) HA! HA! HA! HA!

All react in horror and cower R, *as*

The Demons leap on L. *Laughing as usual, Morac sweeps on dragging the Spider. The Spider pulls away from the Witch and rushes to her parents*

Spider Mother! Father!

The King and Queen hug and kiss the Spider

Queen Oh, Valtina! Alive! Oh, my darling child!

King My daughter! Oh, even as a spider we love you! Our dear child returned to us!

Morac (*scornfully*) HA! HA! HA!
　　　　Enjoy this reunion while you can, you'll soon have cause for sorrow!
　　　　The Royal House of Valador shall never see tomorrow!
　　　　You three I plan to kill forthwith and I shall reign instead!
　　　　I now will cast the demon spell and render you quite dead!
　　　　O, powers of darkness, hark now to me!
　　　　I conjure up thy devilry! . . .

1st Boy (*shouting to the children*) At her, gang! Stop her from casting the spell!

Yelling at the top of their voices, the children rush at Morac. They dance around her, waving their arms and making lots of noise. Morac screams orders to her Demons and they try to restrain the children. During this the 1st Boy pulls the Royal Family downstage R

(*Shouting above the din*) Quick, your majesties. Make a run for it! We'll hold her off as long as we can!

King But——

1st Boy (*pushing them out down* R) RUN!!

The Royal Family run out down R

Morac seeing this rushes to pursue them. The 1st Boy stops her and they struggle. With a terrible cry, she hurls him to the ground. The Demons and children stop struggling and go silent. The 1st Boy crawls to his friends

Morac   SO! You puny little worms! You think you've set them free!
                I'll get them back in half a tick, they'll not escape from me!

Morac is about to sweep down R, *when . . .*

Jack and Molly enter and bar her way. They are followed by half the sailors brandishing cutlasses

Jack (*striking a dramatic pose*) HOLD! STAY! (*He draws his sword*)
Children HURRAY!

With a snarl, Morac rushes to exit down L, *but . . .*

Granfer Fuddlewick leaps on, followed by the other sailors

Granfer (*striking a comic version of Jack's pose*) 'OLD YER STAYS! (*He draws his sword—the blade is only four inches long!*)
Children HURRAY!

The rest of the chorus run on from up R *and* L *and fill the back*

Morac and her Demons discover they are surrounded and hiss and snarl like rats in a trap

Jack Surrender Morac! You are surrounded!
Morac Forward my Demons!
Jack Up boys and at 'em!!

With a great cry, Jack, Granfer and the sailors rush at the Demons. They fight. The children and chorus cheer on Jack and his men. Morac rushes to escape down R, *but finds Molly barring her way. They struggle. The Witch makes a magic pass at Molly and she falls to the ground and lies motionless*

Morac rushes out down L

The Demons are beaten and they run out R *and* L, *wailing in terror and defeat*

Jack, Granfer and the sailors wave their swords in triumph

All HURRAY!

Granfer (*seeing Molly*) Look! What's 'appened to Miss Muffet?
Jack (*rushing forward and kneeling beside Molly*) MOLLY! ... Molly, darling!

The others surge forward and gather around. Jack lifts Molly gently

Molly (*dazed*) Jack ...
Jack Molly ... are you all right?
Molly Yes ... (*She gets to her feet with Jack's help*) I ... MORAC! I ... I tried to stop her, but ... Did she get away?
Jack I'm afraid so!
Molly And Princess Valtina?
1st Boy She escaped with the King and Queen.
Granfer Oi recken the ole Witch be gone after 'em!
Molly Jack, what are we going to do?

Suddenly Dame Drinkup enters briskly from down L. *Flip and Flop follow*

Dame Have no fear, Drinkup's here! Hi, folks!

They greet her without enthusiasm

(*To the audience*) COR! What it is to be popular! (*To the others*) Come on, cheer up! I've got some good news! You'll never guess who we picked up on our way to the party! (*She calls off* L) THIS WAY!

The Gorilla enters carrying a very disgruntled Morac. He carries her to the C

All HURRAY!
Dame I thought you might be pleased to see the poison dwarf!
Morac (*struggling*) You hairy brute! You'll rue this day!
Put me down at once, I say!

The Gorilla lets her drop to the ground with a thud. Everyone laughs. The magic wand falls from Morac's hand and she crawls towards it, but Jack plants his foot on the wand and picks it up

Morac (*leaping to her feet*) My wand! Give me that! (*She claws for the wand*)
Jack (*holding the wand away and pushing Morac back*) Oh, no you don't! I'll take charge of this! In your hands this wand was an instrument of evil! You used its great power to terrorize and destroy! Without it you are helpless!
Dame (*to the audience*) What shall we do with her, kids! Got any ideas?

The audience shout back their blood-thirsty suggestions. Dame Drinkup and the others respond ad lib. Morac cringes at each horrible suggestion

Jack (*at last, calling order*) NO! LISTEN EVERYONE! The best thing to do is make her vanish from the face of the earth completely!

Everyone agrees

(*Holding up the wand*)
O magic wand make things come right,
And all our thanks you'll earn.
Make Morac vanish from our sight,
And never more return!

He points the wand at Morac. The whirring noise is heard and Lights flash across the stage. There is a loud explosion, a blinding flash and a Black-out

   Morac exits

When the Lights return to normal, Morac has vanished from the scene. Everyone cheers

Molly (*with sudden alarm*) Oh, no! This is terrible!

Jack What is it, Molly?

Molly Don't you understand! By destroying Morac we've destroyed Princess Valtina's only chance of returning to normal! Morac was the only one who could change her back! Because of us she'll have to remain a SPIDER FOREVER!

All (*groaning*) Oh, no!

Jack Well, there's nothing else for it! I'll have to bring the Witch back and make her remove the curse! (*He holds up the wand*)
                   O, magic wand, your help we need!
                   Return the Witch with all due speed!

He points the wand at C. Nothing happens. All react

Dame I think the battery's gone flat!

Molly Let's all say it! (*To the audience*) You'll help as well, won't you? Ready! After three—ONE—TWO—THREE!

All   O, magic wand, your help we need!

Audience   Return the Witch with all due speed!

Jack points the wand. Nothing. All are despondent

Dame (*to the audience*) Is there a pint of Heineken in the house?

   There is a flash down R and the Fairy appears

   That's all we need. Hopeless Hester!

Fairy   Good people, do not be downcast,
                   I've come to give some help at last!
                   To take away the curse is simple . . .

Dame   Well, tell us how, you silly pimple!

Fairy   There is no chant or spell to make!
                   It's just the wand you have to break!

Dame (*to Jack*) Well, don't just stand there!
                      BREAK IT! BREAK IT!

Everyone encourages Jack to do so. He tries, but can't break the wand. The Gorilla ambles over and takes the wand from Jack. With a gigantic effort and lots of grunts, it succeeds in snapping the wand in two. Everyone cheers. The Dame holds up the Gorilla's arm like a boxing champion

Suddenly there is loud music, special lighting and a transformation takes place. The ugly backcloth is flown to reveal a beautiful landscape with a shining royal palace in the distance. A rostrum runs across the back with steps in the centre. The grim side wings now show flowers and trees. The whole scene is now brightly lit. All those on stage gape in amazement

Granfer Cor! This beats (*local posh area*).

Fairy   This change of scene is really grand!
                     And still more wonders are at hand!
                     The best surprise is yet to be,
                     Please turn around and you will see!

She waves her wand upstage

Everyone turns to face upstage. A fanfare is heard, then grand entrance music

King Valentine, Queen Valtora and Princess Valtina enter on the rostrum. All three wear sparkling crowns and magnificent robes. They descend the steps and walk slowly downstage waving to the cheering crowd as they pass. Princess Valtina rushes straight to Molly, Jack and Dame Drinkup

Princess My dear friends!

Molly (*delighted*) Oh, Princess! Is it really you?

Dame Who do you think it is—(*pop star or politician*)?

Princess However can I thank you for what you have done. The Witch is gone forever! Our kingdom is beautiful once more and I am back to normal. (*She giggles*) It does seem odd to have only *one* pair of legs again!

King A thousand thanks to you all. Please look upon Valador as your second home.

Queen If there is anything you want, just ask for it. No request is too great for what you have done.

Dame Ta very much, Maj. Let's see! (*Counting on her fingers*) I want a new water bed! A new set of choppers! The latest (*pop group*) album! A new——

Molly (*to the Queen*) No, thank you, your majesty. Your happiness is the only reward we seek.

Dame Huh! You seek for yerself, girl!

Jack There is only one thing we need, your majesty.

King Yes?

Jack A ship to get us home.

King A SHIP! Why, you can have a hundred ships! A thousand ships!

During Dame Drinkup's next few lines Princess Valtina whispers in her father's ear

Dame One's enough, thanks very much! Oh, crumbs! More up and down, up and down! . . . Can't we go home by bus?

King Excuse me, Dame Drinkup, but you won't be going home just yet.

Dame Eh? Why's that, your royal flush?

King My daughter has just informed me that it was your birthday when you set out to rescue her.

Dame (*remembering*) Yeah! It was an' all!

King Well, you must have missed out on your party.

Dame (*to the audience*) 'E's right, y'know.

King Tonight I shall hold a magnificent party in your honour. The whole kingdom shall be invited.

All HURRAY!

Dame (*thrilled to bits*) Ooo! A Royal Beano just for me! That'll be one in the eye for the girls at the Periwinkle (*or local*) W.I.!

Jack (*stepping forward with Molly*) Little Miss Muffet and I have something

to celebrate as well! As soon as we return to England we are going to be
married.

All HURRAY!

Everyone congratulates Molly and Jack. Granfer takes the King to one side

Granfer Will there be any ale at this 'ere party?
King (*laughing*) As much as you can drink!
Granfer (*jumping for joy*) WHOOPEEE!!!

*In his excitement, he grabs Dame Drinkup and kisses her. Everyone roars with
laughter and goes into the song*

18. Song (All)

After the song, a frontcloth is lowered or the tabs close

SCENE 6

Before the party

Tabs, or a frontcloth

Dame Drinkup bounces on from down L

Dame (*to the audience*) WATCH'ER, ME LOVELIES! Well, that's it! All
gone! (*She sighs*) Ahhhh! Come on! (*She encourages them to sigh with her*)
Ahhhh! Did you enjoy it? I thought you did! Oh, you've been a smashin'
audience! The best we've had all night! TA! TA! NIGHT-NIGHT! GOD
BLESS! (*She goes to exit down* R, *blowing kisses to the audience*)

Flip and Flop enter from down L

Flip (*calling to the Dame*) Oy! Rent-a-tent! Where are you going?
Dame (*coming back*) I'm just going to titivate myself for the party.
Flip You've forgotten something, haven't you! (*He whispers in her ear*)
Dame Oh, *yes*! (*She addresses the audience*) My lords, ladies and jellys-
poons! You're all going to sing! Oh, yes, you are! (*Pointing to someone*)
Even *you*! (*Calling off-stage*) FRED! Lock all the doors! Right then! (*To
Flop*) Have you got the doin's?
Flop No, I always stand like this.
Dame (*hitting him*) The words, you fathead! The words of the song these
budding (*pop star or singer*) are goin' to sing!
Flip Here they come now!

*The song-sheet is lowered, or can be brought out by some of the chorus. It is a
very familiar song, a "She'll Be Coming Round The Mountain" type*

Dame (*to the audience*) Right then, you lucky lot of (*local place*) layabouts!
Now's yer chance. You all know this one, don't you? We'll start it off and
you can join in. (*To Conductor or Pianist*) MUSIC, ANDRÉ, PLEASE!

19. Sing-a-Long Song (Dame, Flip, Flop and Audience)

*They have a lot of fun getting the audience to sing. After the song, the song
sheet is flown or removed*

DIDN'T THEY DO WELL! (*To the audience*) Some of you ought to be on that TV show!
Flip Top of the Pops?
Dame NO!—(*popular TV wild life programme*).

The Gorilla enters from down R. *He wears a footman's coat and a white "dicky" front. He carries a dinner gong and beats it loudly*

Dame Look! It's J. Arthur Crank!
Flip That means grub's up! HEY! It must be time for your party!
Dame Well, what are we waitin' for?

The music starts up and they run out down L, *waving and shouting "Ta-ta" and "Bye" to the audience*

The Gorilla gives the audience a stately bow and runs out after them, as ...

The Lights fade to Black-out. Fanfare

SCENE 7

Dame Drinkup's Party—Finale. (The setting for the transformation scene can be used)

All enter for the Finale Walkdown. If more time is needed for the principals' costume changes, the chorus can sing a reprise of No. 18 before the principals enter

After the walkdown, some of the chorus wheel out an enormous birthday cake with lots of candles. Dame Drinkup is about to blow out the candles when the Gorilla bursts through the top of the cake wearing a large, sparkling top hat and a hugh bow tie. All come forward

Jack   And now it's time for us to go.
Molly   We hope you have enjoyed the show.
Flip   We've done our best to make you smile.
Princess And forget your cares awhile.
Fairy   For services rendered I've pass the test!

She shows tiny wings in place of her "L" plate

Grasper   My hopes of wealth have all gone west!
Morac   I'll get you all this time next year!
Granfer (*putting his arm around the Dame*)
              Let's get together! Eh, me dear?
Dame   If that's a proposal, you're gettin' bolder!
Flop   He certainly likes his women older!
Dame   ON WITH THE PARTY! LET'S GET TO THE BUFFET!
              (*To rhyme with Muffet*)
All   GOOD NIGHT AND GOD BLESS FROM LITTLE MISS MUFFET!

20. Final Chorus (All)

CURTAIN

FURNITURE AND PROPERTY LIST

ACT I

SCENE 1

On stage: Harbour backcloth
Rostrum with steps leading to harbour wall
Inn with *Fillet Inn* sign
Cottage wings
Benches and table. *On table:* tankards

Off stage: Trays with tankards **(Barmaids)**
Large gift-wrapped box with pink ribbon bow **(Children)**
Supermarket trolley containing various items, including bottle of toilet
cleaner, toilet roll, packets of sweets **(Dame)**
Tattered smock, black face, pink ribbon bow **(Granfer)**
Top hat **(Grasper)**
Big drum and stick **(Flop)**
Cymbals **(Flip)**
Large picnic hamper **(Dame)**

Personal: **Jack:** sword (required throughout)

SCENE 2

On stage: Tabs or frontcloth

Off stage: Bag of sweets in packets, clicking teeth **(Flop)**
Six-foot pencil **(Flop)**

SCENE 3

On stage: Forest backcloth
Tree wings
Forest ground row
Large picnic hamper

Off stage: Drawn sword **(Jack)**
Blindfold **(Dame)**

Personal: **Granfer:** paper bag, blindfold in pocket
Spider: small medallion on chain (required throughout)

SCENE 4

On stage: Tabs or frontcloth

Off stage: Shopping bag containing rolls of wallpaper **(Dame)**

SCENE 5

On stage: Parlour backcloth
              Parlour wings
              Pasting table
              Step-ladder
              Buckets of "paste"
              Pasting brushes
              Rolls of wallpaper
              Stage cloth

Off stage: Bucket of "paste" **(Dame)**

ACT II

SCENE 1

On stage: Sky cloth
              Ship's bulwarks
              Sails and rigging side wings
              Ship's bridge with steps
              Large sea-chest
              Bales, barrels, piles of rope, etc.
              Buckets, mops, dusters for **Sailors**

Off stage: Broken bits of mast, rigging, etc. **(Stage Management)**
              Ship's wheel **(Granfer)**

Personal: **Granfer:** dummy cat and dummy parrot, sword
              Jack: telescope
              Dame: whistle on ribbon
              Morac: magic wand (required throughout)

SCENE 2

On stage: Tabs or frontcloth

Personal: **Fairy:** wand, "L" plate (required throughout)
              Demons: spears, long rope

SCENE 3

On stage: Seashore backcloth
              Jungle wings
              Jungle ground row
              Tall rock with steps and ledge
              Low flat rock

Personal: **Dame:** rubber fish down costume
              Demons: spears

SCENE 4

On stage: Tabs or frontcloth

Personal: **Demons:** spears

SCENE 5

On stage: Dark Tower backcloth
Dark Tower wings
Stone bench

After transformation on page 51:
Transformation scene backcloth and side wings
Rostrum and steps

Personal: **King, Queen:** manacles
Demons: spears, whip
Sailors: cutlasses
Granfer: sword with very short blade

SCENE 6

On stage: Tabs or frontcloth

Off stage: Song-sheet **(Stage Management** or **Chorus)**
Dinner gong with beater **(Gorilla)**

SCENE 7

On stage: As at end of Scene 5

Off stage: Large trick birthday cake on trolley **(Chorus)**

Personal: **Fairy:** tiny pair of wings in place of "L" plate

LIGHTING PLOT

Property fitting required: nil

Various interior and exterior settings

ACT I, Scene 1

To open: General exterior lighting

| Cue 1 | **Dame:** "See you at the picnic!" **Dame** and **Granfer** exit
Fade to black-out | (Page 12) |

ACT I, Scene 2

To open: General exterior lighting

Cue 2	**Flip:** "Come on down!" *House lights up*	(Page 13)
Cue 3	**Flip** helps children off stage *House lights down*	(Page 13)
Cue 4	**Grasper** chases off **Flip** and **Flop** *Fade to black-out*	(Page 14)

ACT I, Scene 3

To open: General exterior lighting

| Cue 5 | **Flip** and **Flop** exit on the other side
Fade to black-out | (Page 19) |

ACT I, Scene 4

To open: General exterior lighting

Cue 6	**Dame:** ". . . bless her little heart." *Fade to green spot on* **Grasper**	(Page 20)
Cue 7	**Grasper:** "Ah! I have a plan!" *Return to previous lighting*	(Page 21)
Cue 8	**Grasper:** "Give it to *me*! HA! HA! HA!" He exits *Fade to black-out*	(Page 22)

ACT I, Scene 5

To open: General interior lighting
No cues

ACT II, Scene 1

To open: General exterior lighting

Cue 9	After **Song 13.** *Flash of lightning, eerie lights replace general lighting, flickering lights from sea*	(Page 32)
Cue 10	**Demons** fall to their knees, heralding approach of their queen *Flash of lightning*	(Page 32)
Cue 11	**Morac** points wand at **Jack** *Special lighting (strobe if possible) flashes across stage*	(Page 33)
Cue 12	**Morac** lowers wand *Flashing lights fade*	(Page 33)
Cue 13	**Morac** and **Demons** exit *Storm lighting—lightning flashes etc.*	(Page 34)
Cue 14	**Granfer** enters with ship's wheel *Quick black-out*	(Page 34)

ACT II, Scene 2

To open: Dim, eerie lighting

Cue 15	**Demons** leap on from down R and L *Flash of lightning*	(Page 34)
Cue 16	**Fairy** enters *Spot on* **Fairy**	(Page 34)
Cue 17	**Fairy** exits down R *Cut spot*	(Page 35)
Cue 18	**Morac** exits down L *Fade to black-out*	(Page 36)

ACT II, Scene 3

To open: General exterior lighting

Cue 19	**All:** "Ay!" *Flash of lightning, dim and eerie lights replace general lighting*	(Page 42)
Cue 20	**Demons** gather at base of steps *Flash of lightning*	(Page 42)
Cue 21	**Morac** points wand at the group *Dazzling lights flash across stage*	(Page 43)
Cue 22	**Morac** lowers wand *Fade dazzling lights*	(Page 43)
Cue 23	**Demons** exit *Lighting returns to normal*	(Page 43)
Cue 24	**Fairy** enters *Spot on* **Fairy**	(Page 43)
Cue 25	**Fairy:** "... *if* you are lucky!" *Cut spot*	(Page 44)

Cue 26   **Gorilla** exits   (Page 44)
            Fade to black-out

ACT II, SCENE 4

To open: Dim, eerie lighting

Cue 27   **Morac** points wand at **Grasper**   (Page 45)
            Dazzling lights flash across stage, followed by black-out; after
            pause, lights up to previous level

Cue 28   **Flip** and **Flop** exit   (Page 47)
            Fade to black-out

ACT II, SCENE 5

To open: Dim, sinister lighting

Cue 29   **Jack** points wand at **Morac**   (Page 51)
            Dazzling lights flash across stage followed by black-out; after
            pause, lights up to previous level

Cue 30   **Dame:** ". . . a pint of Heineken in the house?"   (Page 51)
            Spot on **Fairy** *as she enters*

Cue 31   **Gorilla** breaks wand. All cheer   (Page 51)
            Transformation scene lighting—brightly lit stage

ACT II, SCENE 6

To open: General lighting

Cue 32   **Gorilla** runs out   (Page 54)
            Fade to black-out

ACT II, SCENE 7

To open: Bright, general lighting

No cues

EFFECTS PLOT

ACT I

Cue 1   **Dame:** "Where's me prezzy? Where is it?"   (Page 6)
Flash and loud explosion (off)

Cue 2   **Grasper:** "... the fabulous—Flip and Flop!"   (Page 8)
Fanfare or drum roll

Cue 3   **Grasper:** "The fabulous Flip and Flop!"   (Page 8)
Repeat Cue 2

Cue 4   **Grasper:** "The fabulous Flip and Flop!"   (Page 8)
Repeat Cue 2

ACT II

Cue 5   **Jack:** "Number one gun! FIRE!!"   (Page 30)
Ship's cannon fires (off)

Cue 6   After **13. Song**   (Page 32)
Tremendous clap of thunder

Cue 7   **Sailor** (*pointing to the back*) LOOK!"   (Page 32)
Weird noises, ground mist

Cue 8   **Demons** fall to their feet, heralding the approach of their
queen   (Page 32)
Roll of thunder

Cue 9   Still laughing, **Morac** descends to deck   (Page 33)
Fade weird noises

Cue 10   **Morac** points wand at **Jack**   (Page 33)
Strange whirring noises

Cue 11   **Morac** lowers wand   (Page 33)
Whirring noises fade

Cue 12   **Morac:** "... and work for me!"   (Page 33)
Monstrous roars and bellowings, off; then fade

Cue 13   **Morac:** "... and truly dead! HA! HA! HA!"   (Page 33)
Blinding flash

Cue 14   **Morac** and **Demons** exit   (Page 34)
Storm effects—thunder, crashing waves, etc.

Cue 15   As Scene 2 opens   (Page 34)
Gradually fade storm effects

Cue 16   **Demons** leap on from down R and L   (Page 34)
Roll of thunder

Cue 17   **Morac:** "... sharks have got 'em! HA! HA! HA!"   (Page 34)
            Flash as **Fairy** *enters*

Cue 18   **All:** "Ay!"   (Page 42)
            Clap of thunder

Cue 19   **Demons** gather at base of steps   (Page 42)
            Roll of thunder

Cue 20   **Morac** points her wand at the group   (Page 43)
            Strange whirring noises

Cue 21   **Morac** lowers wand   (Page 43)
            Fade whirring noises

Cue 22   **Demons** exit   (Page 43)
            Flash as **Fairy** *appears*

Cue 23   **Fairy:** "... *if* you are lucky!"   (Page 44)
            Flash as **Fairy** *exits*

Cue 25   **Morac** points wand at **Grasper**   (Page 45)
            Strange whirring noises; fade during black-out

Cue 26   As Scene 5 opens   (Page 47)
            Weird, spooky noises, then fade

Cue 27   **Jack** points wand at **Morac**   (Page 51)
            *Strange whirring noises followed by loud explosion and blinding
            flash*

Cue 28   During black-out   (Page 51)
            Fade noises

Cue 29   **Dame:** "... of Heineken in the house?"   (Page 51)
            Flash as **Fairy** *enters*

Cue 30   **Gorilla** breaks wand. All cheer   (Page 51)
            Flash for transformation scene

Cue 31   Everyone turns to face upstage   (Page 52)
            Fanfare

Cue 32   **Gorilla** runs out; lights fade to black-out   (Page 54)
            Fanfare

MADE AND PRINTED IN GREAT BRITAIN BY
LATIMER TREND & COMPANY LTD PLYMOUTH

MADE IN ENGLAND